Instant Pot Pro Multi-Cooker Cookbook for Beginners

1001-Day Savory & Foolproof Recipes For Beginners to

Pressure Cook,Slow Cook,Steam,Yogurt Make & Fry For

the Instant Pot Pro Multi-Cooker.

● Sheridan Adrianne

Table of Contents

CHAPTER 1: INSTANT POT PRO MULTI-COOKER BASICS

Advanced technology makes your daily cooking easy and healthy. Most people want to cook healthy and delicious dishes at home. Due to the busy schedule of our lifestyle, it is not possible to give much time for daily cooking. If you are also one of them then Instant Pot Pro Multi-Cooker is one of the best choices for you.

Why use a Instant Pot Pro Multi-Cooker? It all boils down to speed and versatility. By building up steam and, in turn, raising the pressure and temperature, Instant

Pot cookers can get the effects of long braises, boils, and simmers in no time at all. You save loads of cooking time and energy in the process without losing any of the taste and still maintaining texture.

What is the Instant Pot Pro Multi-Cooker?

There are lots of innovative kitchen appliances are available in today's market most of them are multi-functional appliances. Instant Pot Pro Multi-Cooker allow you to prepare a variety of food in a single appliance. This types of appliances do not only save your time and money but also save your kitchen countertop space. Having an Instant Pot Pro Multi-Cooker is like having the size of half of your kitchen in just one machine. This is because it has the ability to grill, bake, cook, fry and do so much more at the push of a button.

Instant Pot Pro Multi-Cooker is an amazing tool to save time and money cooking delicious meals that otherwise would take hours to make. However sometimes we get bored preparing the same meals every day. To make cooking interesting and fun, we have to have variety in our kitchen. In this book you will find the best, hand-picked recipes that you can make with Instant Pot Pro Multi-Cooker. Meals that you will prepare will be absolutely delicious.

The Benefits of Instant Pot Pro Multi-Cooker

The Instant Pot Pro Multi-Cooker has a great choice for every cooking task it helps to make your cooking easy,healthy,and delicious.There are various kinds of benefits of using a Instant Pot cooker some of them are as follows.

- *COOK FOOD FAST.*

Instant Pot Pro Multi-Cooker cuts traditional cooking times by up to 70 percent,making it great for super-quick meals. It greatly decreases typically long cooking times for dishes like beans, thick meats, and stocks, making slow weekend dishes into weekday options.

- *PRESERVE NUTRITION FOR HEALTHY MEALS.*

Because Instant Pot cooking requires less cooking liquid, it's more nutritious than boiling, as fewer minerals leach out of the food and into the liquid. The shorter cooking time also helps preserve the natural vitamins inside the food, making Instant Pot cooking an exceptionally healthy cooking method.

- *SAVES YOUR MONEY*

This is one of the main benefits of Instant Pot Pro Multi-Cooker in which you

can use tougher meat cuts to get into the cheaper price. Slow cooking melts the collagen within meat cuts that make these meats tender and soft after cooking at low temperatures for several hours.Compare to a standard electric oven slow cooker takes very low energy to cook your food even if it takes a long period of cooking time at a very low temperature.There is no energy wastage while cooking food for a long time.

- *MAKE GREAT DISHES WITHOUT THE FUSS.*

Instant Pot Pro Multi-Cooker automatically regulate the pressure and use a timer to control the cooking time. These automated functions make them simpler to use than their stove-top counterparts, and their hands-off functionality make them extra safe and all-around user-friendly. This is an appliance you'll want to keep on your countertop.

- *SAFE TO USE.*

The Instant Pot Pro Multi-Cooker is one of the safest cooking appliance designs to leave to cook for a long period. It is also safe for countertop cooking and can be kept unattended for a long period of time.It never burns your food the auto shut and microprocessor technology makes your slow cooker smarter and safer to cook your food.

- *GO GREEN.*

With a faster cooking time and an efficient use of energy, Instant Pot Pro Multi-Cooker are eco-friendly. When compared to stove-top and other cooking methods, Instant Pot cooking uses two to three times less energy.

There are lots of reasons to love Instant Pot Pro Multi-Cooker, so treat the list of benefits below as just the beginning. As you expand your cooking knowledge and experience, your list will only get longer.

How to Cook Food into Instant Pot Pro Multi-Cooker

Instant Pot Pro Multi-Cooker is very easy to operate, you just need some understandings about functions given over the control panel. It comes with very few touch button settings and anyone can easily operate selecting proper settings. The following step by step guide will help you to operate your Instant Pot Pro Multi-Cooker easily.

- *Clear space on a countertop*

Your Instant Pot Pro Multi-Cooker emits heat so make sure that plenty of space available from all sides of your Instant Pot Pro Multi-Cooker.There is air ventilation available for the room,safety is a priority.

- *Start preparation*

Choose your recipe first,and then preheat the Instant Pot Pro Multi-Cooker as per your recipe needs. Select the function the display will show you preset time and temperature setting. You can also adjust manual time and temperature settings as per recipe needs.

- *Add desire ingredients*

Add all the ingredients like vegetables,sausage,and spices into the cooking pot. Mix all ingredients using spatulas then add liquid into cooker pot, make sure to keep the liquid level below the maximum level.

- *Close lid and Stat cooking*

After adding all the ingredients close the lid properly. Then select function and adjust the time and temperature setting as per recipe needs. Your instant pot starts the cooking process by slowly heating the cooking pot. Relax and leave it until the cooking process is done. After finishing the complete cooking cycle your Instant Pot Pro Multi-Cooker gives beeps and automatically set on KEEP WARM mode until you have to check your food.

- *Cleaning your Instant Pot Pro Multi-Cooker*

After every use,you have to clean your cooking pot with the help of soapy water or you can clean it with the dishwasher.

A Few Tips

- Many pots switch to a "Keep Warm" function after the cook time is over. To avoid overcooking, press Cancel or unplug the pot.

- Don't overfill the pot. For foods that expand during cooking, like beans, don't fill it more than half full. For other foods, don't fill it more than two-thirds full.

- When you open the lid, open it away from yourself and others. Similarly, when you release the pressure, keep your hands and face away from the hot steam.

- To reduce your sauce and concentrate its flavor, simmer the liquid for a few minutes until it reaches the desired consistency.

- Something other than steam comes out of the steam release handle. Quickly turn the handle to the sealing position and allow the pressure to release naturally.

- The silicone ring tends to absorb cooking odors. Remove and wash it after every use, and let it dry thoroughly.If you are particularly bothered by the smell, you can use separate rings for sweet and savory dishes.

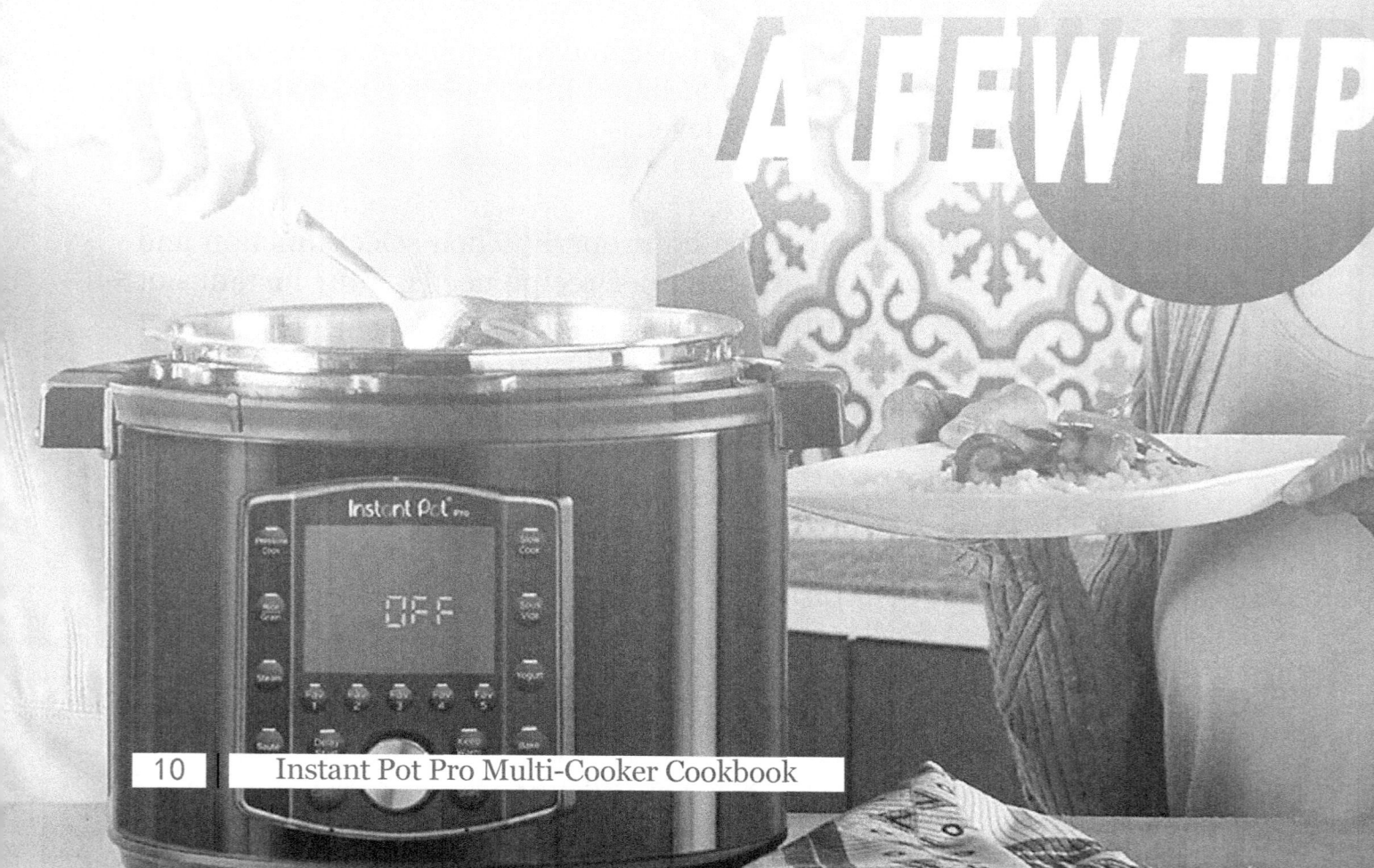

What to Expect From the Rest of This Book

With an Instant Pot Pro Multi-Cooker, even the most inept cook can get a decent meal out of it because all you need to do is toss in the ingredients and the pot does the cooking for you. That being said, you still want to be able to enjoy gourmet meals that are delicious and homemade and this book helps you achieve exactly that. You get a variety of instant pot food ideas that only requires you to combine certain ingredients together and enjoy a bust of flavor when it is done.

You may need to put in some work here and there especially when it comes to preparing the ingredients before putting it into the pot. But these are simple ideas and have been created to suit a variety of food preferences. So whether you are vegan or vegetarian or you are craving something a little more exotic, there is something for you in this book.

All the recipes in this book are pretty simple to prepare and are written in a clear and easy to follow fashion. You won't have to wonder what to do next, these recipes will guide you every step of the way in order to make the tastiest pressure cooker meals ever.

Instant Pot Pro Multi-Cooker FAQs

FAQ # 1 –The unit has started pressure cooking. Can I still move it?

No, it is NOT recommended that you move the unit once pressure cooking has started.

FAQ # 2 –Is the outside of the Instant Pot Pro Multi-Cooker safe to touch when cooking?

The outside unit of the Instant Pot Pro Multi-Cooker will get hot so be careful when touching anything other than the control panel, the handle on the lid, and the exterior handles.

FAQ # 3 – How often should I clean the silicone ring and how?

It is recommended that you clean the silicone ring after every use. Wash the silicone ring in warm, soapy water. If cleaning the silicone ring in the dishwasher, place it on the top rack.

CHAPTER 2: BREAKFAST

Healthy Carrot Cake Oatmeal

Prep Time: 5 Minutes
Cook Time: 4 Minutes
Serves: 4

Ingredients:

- 2 cups gluten-free steel cut oats
- 8 carrots, shredded
- ½ cup raisins
- ½ cup unsweetened shredded coconut
- ¼ cup chopped pecans
- 2 teaspoons vanilla extract
- 2 teaspoons lemon zest
- 1 teaspoon ground cinnamon
- ¼ teaspoon Celtic sea salt or kosher salt
- 4 tablespoons maple syrup

Directions:

1. Use pressure cooker to mix together 4 cups of water, the oats, and carrots. Close the hood in place and set to High pressure for 4 minutes.
2. Once it is done, let the pressure release naturally for 15 minutes; manually release any remaining pressure.
3. Cautiously open the lid and whisk in the raisins, coconut, pecans, vanilla, lemon zest, cinnamon, and salt.
4. Drizzle 1 tablespoon of maple syrup on the top of each serving.

Nutritional Value (Amount per Serving):

- Calories: 275
- Fat: 8.15g
- Carbs: 59.22g
- Protein: 10.1g

Easy Eggs In Purgatory

Prep Time: 5 Minutes
Cook Time: 20 Minutes
Serves: 4

Ingredients:

- 2 tablespoons extra-virgin olive oil
- 6 garlic cloves, minced
- 4 cups fresh baby spinach
- 4 cups Super Simple Marinara
- 2 teaspoons red pepper flakes
- 8 large eggs
- 2 tablespoons chopped fresh parsley
- 1 whole-grain baguette, for serving

Directions:

1. Preheat the oven to 350°F.
2. In a large ovenproof skillet with the setting of medium heat, heat the olive oil.
3. Add the garlic. Cook for 2 to 3 minutes until fragrant. Stir in the spinach, marinara, and red pepper flakes. Cook for 2 to 4 minutes, or until the spinach wilts.
4. Using a spoon, create 8 small wells in the sauce. Crack 1 egg into each well. Takethe skillet to the oven. Bake for 10 to 12 and wait the eggs get set.
5. Sprinkle with the parsley and serve with the baguette.

Nutritional Value (Amount per Serving):

- Calories: 172
- Fat: 13.25g
- Carbs: 6.89g
- Protein: 7.22g

Simple Potato Breakfast Bowls

Prep Time: 5 Minutes
Cook Time: 8 Minutes
Serves: 6

Ingredients:

- 5 medium sweet potatoes, peeled and diced
- ½ cup canned full-fat coconut milk
- 1 teaspoon vanilla extract
- 1½ cups fresh blueberries, or frozen and thawed
- 1 teaspoon ground cinnamon

Directions:

1. Use your pressure cooker to mix together the sweet potatoes and 1 cup of water. Close the hood in place and set at High pressure for 8 minutes.
2. Once it is done, manually release the pressure.
3. Cautiously remove the hood and pour the coconut milk and vanilla. Taking your large spoon to stir or mash the potatoes until creamy.
4. Put ¼ cup of blueberries and a sprinkle of cinnamon on the top of each serving with.

Nutritional Value (Amount per Serving):

- Calories: 201
- Fat: 5.16g
- Carbs: 37.96g
- Protein: 2.62g

Healthy Apple Cinnamon Buns

Prep Time: 15 Minutes

Cook Time: 15 Minutes

Serves: 6

Ingredients:

- 10 ounces Pizza Dough, or store-bought whole-wheat dough
- All-purpose or white whole-wheat flour, for preparing the work surface
- 1 tablespoon cold unsalted butter
- 2 apples, cored
- 1 tablespoon ground cinnamon
- 1 tablespoon sugar
- ¼ teaspoon Celtic sea salt or kosher salt

Directions:

1. Take the dough from the refrigerator 5 to 10 minutes and then take the chill off for using it.
2. Lightly flour a work surface. Put a rolling pin for rolling the dough into a 12-by-8-inch rectangle. Grind the butter into an even layer covering the dough; retry the procedures again with the apples. Sprinkle evenly with the cinnamon, sugar, and salt.
3. Starting at one of the long sides, tightly roll the dough into a cylinder for shape. Slice the cylinder crosswise into 6 rounds.
4. Put the buns in your air fryer's basket. Fry at 325°F for 12 to 15 minutes, orwait and see the golden tops with thoroughly cooked dough.

Nutritional Value (Amount per Serving):

- Calories: 385
- Fat: 2.4g
- Carbs: 80.99g
- Protein: 10.61g

Easy Smoked Salmon Frittata

Prep Time: 10 Minutes
Cook Time: 20 Minutes
Serves: 4

Ingredients:

- 1 tablespoon extra-virgin olive oil
- 1 russet potato, diced
- 1 onion, diced
- ¼ cup Garden Vegetable Stock, or store-bought low-sodium vegetable stock
- 4 large eggs
- 2 large egg whites
- 2 tablespoons fat-free plain Greek yogurt
- 2 ounces smoked salmon, chopped
- 1 tablespoon fresh dill, chopped

Directions:

1. Preheat the oven to 450°F.
2. Use an ovenproof skillet and set for medium-high heat for heating the olive oil.
3. Add the potato and onion. Cook for 5 minutes and wait the onion to get softened and the potato to get brown.
4. Pour in the vegetable stock. Simmer for about 5 minutes when the potatoes are well cooked and the liquid is totally absorbed.
5. Use your medium bowl to stir in the eggs, egg whites, and yogurt. Pour the egg mixture into the skillet. Top evenly with the salmon. Bake for 8 to 10 minutes, and wait the frittata get lightly browned and fluffy. Top with the dill.

Nutritional Value (Amount per Serving):

- Calories: 196
- Fat: 7.45g
- Carbs: 22.67g
- Protein: 10.31g

Sweet "Egg In A Hole" With Potato

Prep Time: 5 Minutes
Cook Time: 20 Minutes
Serves: 4

Ingredients:

- 1 large sweet potato, cut lengthwise into 4 (¼-inch-thick) planks
- 1 tablespoon extra-virgin olive oil
- 4 large eggs
- Celtic sea salt or kosher salt
- Freshly ground black pepper

Directions:

1. Preheat the oven to 450°F.
2. Prepare a 3-inch round cookie cutter or sharp knife for digging a hole in the center of each sweet potato plank. Use olive oil to rub both sides of the potatoes then arrange them on a sheet pan. Bake for 15 minutes and wait the bottoms to caramelize.
3. Flip the potatoes. Crack 1 egg into each hole. Bake for another 5 minutes and wait the eggs to get set. Season to taste with salt and pepper.

Nutritional Value (Amount per Serving):

- Calories: 110
- Fat: 6.13g
- Carbs: 9.93g
- Protein: 3.68g

Exotic Dutch Baby Pancake With Sliced Strawberries

Prep Time: 10 Minutes

Cook Time: 25 Minutes

Serves: 4

Ingredients:

- 1 pint fresh strawberries, trimmed and sliced
- 3 tablespoons plus 1 teaspoon sugar, divided
- 3 large eggs
- ⅔ cup milk
- Zest of 1 lemon
- ¼ teaspoon Celtic sea salt or kosher salt
- ⅔ cup white whole-wheat flour
- 1 tablespoon unsalted butter
- 2 tablespoons sliced almonds
- Maple syrup, for serving (optional)

Directions:

1. Preheat the oven to 400°F.
2. Use your bowl to combine well the strawberries and 1 teaspoon of sugar. Set aside.
3. Use another bowl to stir in the eggs and milk until smooth. Add the lemon zest, the 3 tablespoons of sugar left as well as salt. Stir well to combine and slowly combine the flour to form a thin, smooth batter.
4. Put the butter in a 9-inch ovenproof skillet and then put all of them in the oven for 2 to 3 minutes, and wait the butter to melt. rotate the skillet to coat it with melted butter. Pour the batter into the skillet.
5. Put the pan to the oven again and bake for 20 minutes, and wait the Dutch baby get puffed and golden brown. Take from the oven and put aside for cooling for a few minutes—the pancake will deflate as it cools.
6. Decorate the Dutch baby with the strawberries and almonds on its top. Serve with maple syrup (if using).

Nutritional Value (Amount per Serving):

- Calories: 256
- Fat: 7.46g
- Carbs: 41.99g
- Protein: 6.36g

Yummy Morning Granola

Prep Time: 5 Minutes
Cook Time: 20 Minutes
Serves: 6

Ingredients:

- 2½ cups rolled oats
- ½ cup maple syrup
- ½ cup chopped walnuts
- ¼ cup unsweetened shredded coconut
- 1 large egg white, beaten
- ¼ cup chia or hemp seeds, or a combination
- Zest of 1 lemon
- Pinch Celtic sea salt
- ½ cup dried cranberries (reduced-sugar if you can find them)

Directions:

1. Preheat the oven to 300°F.
2. Use a large bowl to mix together the oats, maple syrup, walnuts, coconut, egg white, and seeds. Combine well until they are thoroughly incorporated. Pour onto a sheet pan. Bake for 20 minutes.
3. Stir in the lemon zest, salt, and cranberries.

Nutritional Value (Amount per Serving):

- Calories: 318
- Fat: 13g
- Carbs: 56.22g
- Protein: 11.63g

Daily Sheet Pan Bacon Eggs

Prep Time: 10 Minutes
Cook Time: 30 Minutes
Serves: 4

Ingredients:

- 8 sugar-free bacon slices
- 1 russet potato, diced
- ½ green bell pepper, seeded and diced
- ½ onion, diced
- 1 tablespoon extra-virgin olive oil
- 1 teaspoon dried parsley
- Celtic sea salt or kosher salt
- Freshly ground black pepper
- 8 large eggs

Directions:

1. Preheat the oven to 400°F. Line a sheet pan with parchment paper.
2. Place the bacon in a single layer for the half of the sheet pan prepared in advance. Distribute the potato, green bell pepper, and onion on the other side and sprinkle the potatoes with the olive oil and take the parsley, salt, and pepper for seasoning. Bake for 20 minutes. Stir the vegetables.
3. Crack the eggs over the potatoes. Bake for another 8 to 10 minutes and wait the eggs to get cooked as you like. Season to taste with salt and pepper.

Nutritional Value (Amount per Serving):

- Calories: 216
- Fat: 10.7g
- Carbs: 22.03g
- Protein: 8.16g

Exquisite Air-Fried Stuffed Apples

Prep Time: 10 Minutes
Cook Time: 13 Minutes
Serves: 4

Ingredients:

- 4 apples
- 1 teaspoon ground cinnamon
- ¼ cup rolled oats
- 2 tablespoons chopped pecans
- Pinch Celtic sea salt or kosher salt
- ½ teaspoon maple syrup
- 2 teaspoons unsalted butter

Directions:

1. Slice the top off each apple. Prepare a paring knife in advance and remove the core. Do not cut all the way through the bottom of the apples. Spread the inside of the apples with the cinnamon.
2. Use a prepared bowl to combine well the oats, pecans, and salt. Separate the filling among the apples. Sprinkle with the syrup andput ½ teaspoon of butter on the top of the apple.
3. Place the apples in your air fryer's basket in order. Fry at 350°f for 13 minutes.

Nutritional Value (Amount per Serving):

- Calories: 149
- Fat: 4.61g
- Carbs: 30.55g
- Protein: 1.91g

Homemade Sausage Egg Scramble

Prep Time: 5 Minutes
Cook Time: 15 Minutes
Serves: 4

Ingredients:

- 1 tablespoon extra-virgin olive oil
- 1 onion, chopped
- 1 bell pepper, any color, chopped
- 2 breakfast sausage links, sliced
- 6 large eggs, beaten
- 2 cups fresh baby spinach

Directions:

1. Use a large skillet over medium heat to heat the olive oil.
2. Put the onion and bell pepper. Cook for 3 to 5 minutes, or until softened.
3. Add the sausage. Cook for 3 to 4 minutes to brown.
4. Whisk in the eggs. Cook for 3 to 4 minutes with constant whisk and stir. Wait the eggs to get set but still creamy.
5. Add the spinach, stirring until wilted.

Nutritional Value (Amount per Serving):

- Calories: 147
- Fat: 10.91g
- Carbs: 5.31g
- Protein: 7.17g

All-Time Favorite Butternut Squash Hash Eggs

Prep Time: 10 Minutes
Cook Time: 25 Minutes
Serves: 4

Ingredients:

- 1 tablespoon extra-virgin olive oil
- 1 onion, diced
- 2 garlic cloves, minced
- 1 butternut squash (about 2 pounds), peeled and diced
- 1 red potato, diced
- ½ cup apple cider
- 1 cup chopped Swiss chard
- 4 large eggs
- 2 tablespoons fresh oregano leaves
- Celtic sea salt or kosher salt
- Freshly ground black pepper

Directions:

1. Preheat the oven to 400°F.
2. Use a large ovenproof skillet and set for medium-high heat for heating the olive oil.
3. Add the onion and garlic. Cook for 3 or 4 minutes until softened.
4. Add the squash, red potato, and cider together. Simmer for 10 minutes and wait the vegetables to get softened and the cider is absorbed.
5. Stir in the chard. Using a spoon and make 4 wells in the hash. Crack 1 egg into each well. Remove the skillet to the oven and bake for 10 minutes, or until the eggs are set.
6. Spread with the oregano and season. Enjoy with salt and pepper.

Nutritional Value (Amount per Serving):

- Calories: 277
- Fat: 6.56g
- Carbs: 51.75g
- Protein: 7.65g

Combined Berry French Toast Casserole

Prep Time: 15 Minutes
Cook Time: 40 Minutes
Serves: 6

Ingredients:

- 8 large egg whites
- 1½ cups lite coconut milk
- ¼ cup maple syrup, plus more for serving (optional)
- 1 teaspoon vanilla extract
- 2 teaspoons ground cinnamon
- 12 slices whole-wheat bread, cut into 1-inch cubes (about 6 cups)
- 2 cups mixed fresh berries, such as strawberries and blueberries

Directions:

1. Preheat the oven to 350°F.
2. Use a large bowl to stir in the egg whites, coconut milk, maple syrup, vanilla, and cinnamon until well mixed.
3. Place the bread cubes in your Dutch oven. Spread the liquid ingredients over the bread and whisk for mixing. Mix in the berries. Let sit for 10 minutes.
4. Bake, uncovered, for 30 to 40 minutes and wait all the liquid to get absorbed and the casserole's top to get lightly browned and crispy.
5. Transfer from the oven and cool it for 5 minutes. Serve with additional syrup (if using).

Nutritional Value (Amount per Serving):

- Calories: 515
- Fat: 20.05g
- Carbs: 75.16g
- Protein: 13.71g

Sweet Banana Bread

Prep Time: 10 Minutes
Cook Time: 1 Hour 15 Minutes
Serves: 4

Ingredients:

- Nonstick cooking spray, for preparing the cake pan
- ¼ cup packed light brown sugar
- ¼ cup granulated sugar
- 1 large egg
- ½ cup fat-free plain Greek yogurt
- ½ teaspoon vanilla extract
- 1 cup plus 1 tablespoon white whole-wheat flour
- ½ teaspoon baking soda
- ¼ teaspoon Celtic sea salt or kosher salt
- 2 very ripe bananas, peeled
- ¼ cup chopped walnuts

Directions:

1. Use cooking spray to cover a 6-inch cake pan and set aside.
2. Use a large bowl to stir iin the brown and granulated sugars and egg until smooth.
3. Stir in the yogurt and vanilla.
4. Lightly stir in the flour, baking soda, and salt to get a very thick batter.
5. Add the bananas. Take a heavy spoon for grind the bananas against the side of the bowl and mix well into the batter. Fold in the walnuts. Pour the batter into the prepared pan and cover with a paper towel casually and use the foil to wrap the whole pan.
6. Put a wire rack in the bottom of your pressure cooker. Pour in 1 cup of water. Put the cake pan over the rack. Close the hood in place and set to High pressure for 1 hour and 15 minutes.

7. Once it is done, manually release the pressure.
8. Cautiously remove the lid and the bread. Let the bread cool before unwrapping.

Nutritional Value (Amount per Serving):

- Calories: 268
- Fat: 5.21g
- Carbs: 50.12g
- Protein: 6.23g

Healthy Peaches Cream Quinoa Bowls

Prep Time: 5 Minutes
Cook Time: 1 Minute
Serves: 4

Ingredients:

- 1½ cups white quinoa, rinsed well
- 1½ cups unsweetened coconut milk, or almond milk
- 1½ cups water
- 2 peaches, chopped
- 1 tablespoon honey
- 1 teaspoon vanilla extract
- Pinch Celtic sea salt or kosher salt

Directions:

1. Use prepared pressure cooker to mix together the quinoa, coconut milk, water, peaches, honey, vanilla, and salt. Close the hood in place and set to High pressure for 1 minute.
2. When the cook time runs out, ensure the pressure release naturally for 10 minutes and then release any remaining pressure. Carefully remove the lid.

Nutritional Value (Amount per Serving):

- Calories: 558
- Fat: 25.46g
- Carbs: 76.47g
- Protein: 11.67g

CHAPTER 3: MEATLESS MAINS

Easy Curried Chickpea Stew

Prep Time: 10 Minutes
Cook Time: 10 Minutes
Serves: 6

Ingredients:

- 1 tablespoon unsalted butter
- 1 onion, chopped
- 1 tablespoon grated peeled fresh ginger
- 4 garlic cloves, minced
- 2 (15-ounce) cans chickpeas, drained
- 1 (15-ounce) can diced fire-roasted tomatoes
- 1 cup cauliflower florets
- 1 tablespoon garam masala
- ½ cup heavy (whipping) cream
- 1 teaspoon freshly squeezed lime juice
- Celtic sea salt or kosher salt

Directions:

1. Use your pressure cooker and pick up Sauté before place the butter in the cooker to melt.
2. Add the onion, ginger, and garlic. Cook for 3 minutes, or until softened.
3. Add the chickpeas, tomatoes, cauliflower, and garam masala. Close the hood in place and set your appliance to High pressure for 6 minutes.
4. When the cook time runs out, manually release the pressure.
5. Cautiously remove the hood and whisk in the heavy cream and lime juice. Season to taste with salt.

Nutritional Value (Amount per Serving):

- Calories: 187
- Fat: 7.53g
- Carbs: 24.38g
- Protein: 7.33g

Delicious Chimichurri Pasta

Prep Time: 20 Minutes
Cook Time: 10 Minutes
Serves: 4

Ingredients:

- Celtic sea salt or kosher salt
- 8 ounces whole-wheat pasta
- 1 pound asparagus, woody ends trimmed, cut into 1-inch pieces
- ½ cup Chimichurri Sauce
- 2 cups fresh baby spinach, chopped
- ½ pint grape tomatoes, quartered
- 2 ounces crumbled feta cheese
- Freshly ground black pepper

Directions:

1. Prepare a dutch oven with salted water to a boil over high heat. Put the pasta into it and cook in line with the package directions until al dente. Two minutes before the pasta is completed, you can add the asparagus. Once the pasta is al dente, drain and clean with cold water.
2. Put the pasta and asparagus to the empty pot. Whisk in the chimichurri sauce, baby spinach, tomatoes, and feta and incorporate well. Season to taste with salt and pepper.

Nutritional Value (Amount per Serving):

- Calories: 165
- Fat: 6.1g
- Carbs: 20.39g
- Protein: 11.3g

Lighter Falafel With Drained Chickpeas

Prep Time: 10 Minutes
Cook Time: 12 Minutes Per Batch
Serves: 4

Ingredients:

- 2 (15-ounce) cans chickpeas, drained
- 1 onion, grated
- 4 garlic cloves, grated
- ¼ cup fresh parsley, chopped
- 1 teaspoon ground cumin
- 1 teaspoon extra-virgin olive oil
- Olive oil cooking spray, for preparing the falafel

Directions:

1. Prepare a large resealable plastic bag in advance and use it to combine the chickpeas, onion, garlic, parsley, cumin, and olive oil. Seal the bag and massage all the objects manually for breaking the chickpeas and incorporate everything into a thick paste. Divide the mixture into 16 tablespoon-size balls and put them on your work surface and flatten slightly. Coat with olive oil cooking spray.
2. Distribute them into batches and put the patties into your air fryer's basket in a single layer in order. Fry at 370°f for 6 minutes per side.

Nutritional Value (Amount per Serving):

- Calories: 200
- Fat: 4.23g
- Carbs: 32.55g
- Protein: 9.62g

Flavorful Italian Eggplant Stacks

Prep Time: 15 Minutes
Cook Time: 20 Minutes
Serves: 4

Ingredients:

- Extra-virgin olive oil, for preparing the sheet pan
- 1 large eggplant, cut into 12 rounds, about ¼ inch thick
- 1 large tomato, cut into 8 rounds, about ¼ inch thick
- 1 large egg, beaten
- Freshly ground black pepper
- ½ cup seasoned Italian bread crumbs
- 1 (4-ounce) fresh mozzarella cheese log or ball, cut into 8 slices
- 8 fresh basil leaves

Directions:

1. Preheat the oven to 450°F. Place a sheet pan with aluminum foil and sprinkle the foil with olive oil.
2. Place the eggplant and tomato slices in order in a single layer on the sheet pan prepared in advance. Use the beaten egg to rub the eggplant and the pepper for seasoning Spread the eggplant with the bread crumbs. Bake for 20 minutes.
3. Put 1 slice of roasted tomato over 4 eggplant slices. Put 1 slice of mozzarella and 1 basil leaf on each tomato. Put another slice of eggplant, tomato, mozzarella, and 1 basil leaf as well as one last eggplant slice over each stack.

Nutritional Value (Amount per Serving):

- Calories: 188
- Fat: 13.08g
- Carbs: 13.65g
- Protein: 6.02g

Easy-Made Pumpkin Lentil Chili

Prep Time: 5 Minutes
Cook Time: 10 Hours
Serves: 6

Ingredients:

- 1 (15-ounce) can pumpkin purée
- 1 cup dried lentils
- 1 (15-ounce) can low-sodium black beans, drained
- 1 (15-ounce) can diced fire-roasted tomatoes
- 2½ cups Garden Vegetable Stock, or low-sodium store-bought vegetable stock
- 1 onion, chopped
- 1 green bell pepper, chopped
- 1 carrot, chopped
- 2 tablespoons gluten-free chili powder
- Celtic sea salt or kosher salt

Directions:

1. Use prepared slow cooker to mix together the pumpkin, lentils, black beans, tomatoes, vegetable stock, onion, green bell pepper, carrot, and chili powder.
2. Close the hood and set it to low heat. Cook for 10 hours and wait the lentils to get soft. Season to taste with salt.

Nutritional Value (Amount per Serving):

- Calories: 865
- Fat: 33.67g
- Carbs: 113.48g
- Protein: 37.47g

Healthy Mushroom Farro "Stroganoff"

Prep Time: 5 Minutes
Cook Time: 30 Minutes
Serves: 4

Ingredients:

- 1 tablespoon extra-virgin olive oil
- 1 onion, thinly sliced
- 8 ounces cremini mushrooms, sliced
- 1 tablespoon peppercorns
- ¾ cup dry sherry
- 2 cups Garden Vegetable Stock, or low-sodium store-bought vegetable stock
- 1 cup pearled farro
- ¼ cup sour cream

Directions:

1. Use a large skillet over medium heat to heat the olive oil.
2. When the oil gets hot, add the onion. Cook for another 5 minutes, or until softened.
3. Add the mushrooms and peppercorns. Cook for another 5 minutes, or until deeply browned.
4. Add the sherry. Cook for 2 to 3 minutes, and wait it to get nearly dissolved.
5. Pour in the vegetable stock and place the mixture to a boil.
6. Add the farro. Cook for 15 minutes and wait the farro to get tender and the liquid to get absorbed. Serve topped with the sour cream.

Nutritional Value (Amount per Serving):

- Calories: 460
- Fat: 6.68g
- Carbs: 98.43g
- Protein: 12.27g

Sweet Creamy Tomato Soup With Farro

Prep Time: 10 Minutes
Cook Time: 8 Hours
Serves: 4

Ingredients:

- 1 (28-ounce) can crushed fire-roasted tomatoes
- ½ cup pearled farro
- 4 garlic cloves, grated
- 1 onion, grated
- 1 carrot, grated
- 2 cups Garden Vegetable Stock, or low-sodium store-bought vegetable stock
- 2 ounces goat cheese
- 2 tablespoons fresh basil, thinly sliced
- Celtic sea salt or kosher salt

Directions:

1. Use the slow cooker to mix together the tomatoes, farro, garlic, onion, carrot, and vegetable stock.
2. Close the hood and set it to low heat. Cook for 8 hours.
3. Whisk in the goat cheese and basil and incorporate well. Season to taste with salt.

Nutritional Value (Amount per Serving):

- Calories: 206
- Fat: 5.95g
- Carbs: 31.31g
- Protein: 9.01g

Tasteful Taco Veggie Burgers Fries

Prep Time: 10 Minutes
Cook Time: 40 To 45 Minutes
Serves: 4

Ingredients:

- 2 russet potatoes, halved lengthwise, each half cut into 6 wedges
- 2 tablespoons extra-virgin olive oil
- Celtic sea salt or kosher salt
- 1 cup drained canned low-sodium black beans
- 1 carrot, grated
- ½ cup walnuts, finely chopped
- ¼ cup grated onion
- 1 (25-ounce) packet taco seasoning
- 4 slices Cheddar cheese (optional)
- 4 hamburger rolls, or lettuce leaves
- 1 avocado, sliced

Directions:

1. Preheat the oven to 400°F.
2. Place the potato wedges in a single layer in a well-managed well on one side of a sheet pan. Fling with the olive oil and season with salt as you like.
3. Use a medium bowl together with a heavy wooden spoon to break and grind the black beans. Whisk in the carrot, walnuts, onion, and taco seasoning and combine well. Separate the mixture into 4 patties and put them on the other side of the sheet pan.
4. Bake for 35 to 40 minutes, flipping the burgers in-between the cooking time. Make burger get topped with 1 slice of cheese (if using) and then put them to the oven for another 2 to 3 minutes to melt the cheese.
5. Serve the burgers on a roll or in lettuce leaves as you like, topped with the avocado.

Nutritional Value (Amount per Serving):

- Calories: 827
- Fat: 28.3g
- Carbs: 136.55g
- Protein: 21.28g

Yummy Potato Fritters With Chipotle Sauce

Prep Time: 10 Minutes
Cook Time: 15 Minutes
Serves: 4

Ingredients:

- 2 sweet potatoes, grated
- 3 cups fresh baby spinach, chopped
- 1 shallot, minced
- 2 large eggs, beaten
- 1 large egg white, beaten
- ½ cup all-purpose flour
- 2 or 3 tablespoons coconut oil, divided
- Celtic sea salt
- ½ cup fat-free plain Greek yogurt
- 1 chipotle in adobo, minced
- 1 tablespoon freshly squeezed lime juice

Directions:

1. Line a plate with paper towels.
2. Use a large bowl to mix together the grated sweet potatoes, spinach, shallot, eggs, egg white, and flour. Combine well for incorporate.
3. Use a large skillet and set medium-high model to melt 1 tablespoon of coconut oil.
4. Scoop in ½-cup portions of batter (3 or 4 fritters usually need 1 can without overcrowding the skillet). Fry for 2 minutes per side and remove to the plate and spread with salt.
5. Pour another tablespoon of coconut oil to the skillet and redo the step 4, continuing to add coconut oil before each batch and make sure all the batter runs out.
6. Use a small bowl to whisk and combine together the yogurt, chipotle, and lime juice.

7.Serve the sweet potato fritters together with the chipotle dipping sauce.

Nutritional Value (Amount per Serving):

- Calories: 228
- Fat: 11.37g
- Carbs: 23.65g
- Protein: 10.22g

Stylish Tofu With Peanut Sauce

Prep Time: 5 Minutes
Cook Time: 8 Minutes Per Batch
Serves: 4

Ingredients:

- 4 cups fresh broccoli florets
- 1 red bell pepper, thinly sliced
- 14 ounces extra-firm tofu, cut into 1-inch cubes
- 1 tablespoon cornstarch
- ¾ cup canned full-fat coconut milk
- ¼ cup smooth peanut butter
- 1 tablespoon grated peeled fresh ginger
- 1 tablespoon low-sodium soy sauce
- 1 tablespoon freshly squeezed lime juice
- Celtic sea salt or kosher salt
- 4 tablespoons chopped peanuts

Directions:

1. Different size of the air fryer requires to work in batches. Use the air fryer's basket to mix together the broccoli and red bell pepper in a single layer.
2. Use a large bowl to mix together the tofu and cornstarch. Toss to coat. Place the tofu in a single layer over the broccoli and bell pepper. Fry at 390°F for 8 minutes.
3. When the stir-fry cooks, use a large bowl to stir together the coconut milk, peanut butter, ginger, soy sauce, and lime juice. Season to taste with salt.
4. Add the cooked vegetables and tofu to the peanut sauce and fling for well coating.
5. Put 1 tablespoon of chopped peanuts over each serving.

Nutritional Value (Amount per Serving):

- Calories: 445
- Fat: 32.75g
- Carbs: 21.06g
- Protein: 24.12g

Exotic Fajita Burrito Bowls

Prep Time: 5 Minutes
Cook Time: 15 Minutes
Serves: 6

Ingredients:

- 1 cup uncooked long-grain brown rice
- 1 (16-ounce) can low-sodium pinto beans, undrained
- 1 cup Garden Vegetable Stock, or low-sodium store-bought vegetable stock
- 2 green bell peppers, sliced
- 2 red onions, sliced
- 1 teaspoon gluten-free chili powder
- 6 ounces shredded pepper Jack cheese
- 2 plum tomatoes, diced
- 1 jalapeño pepper, seeded and minced
- ¼ cup fresh cilantro, chopped

Directions:

1. Use pressure cooker to mix together the brown rice, pinto beans, vegetable stock, green bell peppers, red onions, and chili powder. Close the hood in place and set the model to High pressure for 15 minutes.
2. When the cook time runs out, let the pressure release naturally.
3. Scoop ½ cup of the rice filling into a dish and put cheese, tomato, jalapeño, and cilantro over the top as desired.

Nutritional Value (Amount per Serving):

- Calories: 314
- Fat: 10.16g
- Carbs: 43.03g
- Protein: 13.78g

Healthy Eggplant Asparagus Stir-Fry

Prep Time: 15 Minutes
Cook Time: 15 Minutes
Serves: 6

Ingredients:

- ½ cup low-sodium soy sauce
- ⅓ cup clover honey
- 2 teaspoons cornstarch
- 2 teaspoons grated peeled fresh ginger
- 6 garlic cloves, minced
- ¼ teaspoon red pepper flakes (optional)
- 4 ounces dry rice noodles
- 2 tablespoons extra-virgin olive oil
- 2 pounds eggplant, peeled and diced
- 1 pound asparagus, woody ends trimmed, cut into 1-inch pieces
- ¼ cup cashews, chopped

Directions:

1. Use a small bowl to mix together the soy sauce, honey, cornstarch, ginger, garlic, and red pepper flakes (if using). Stir well to combine and incorporate. Set aside.
2. Usea large deep skillet and adjust to high heat. Pour 4 cups of water to a boil. Add the rice noodles. Cook for 2 minutes until tender. Drain and rinse with cold water. Set aside.
3. Transfer the skillet to high heat and make the olive oil get heated
4. Once the oil is hot, add the eggplant. Cook for 3 minutes.
5. Add the asparagus and ¼ cup of water. Cook for 2 minutes and stirring for several times, or wait the eggplant to get tender and the water to get evaporated.
6. Pour in the stir-fry sauce and cook for another 1 minute to reduce.
7. Transfer the skillet from the heat and whisk in the rice noodles. Top with the cashews.

Nutritional Value (Amount per Serving):

- Calories: 283
- Fat: 8.21g
- Carbs: 48.86g
- Protein: 7.8g

Light Corn Quinoa Chowder

Prep Time: 10 Minutes
Cook Time: 25 Minutes
Serves: 4

Ingredients:

- 2 tablespoons extra-virgin olive oil
- 1 onion, chopped
- 2 celery stalks, thinly sliced
- 1 red bell pepper, chopped
- Celtic sea salt or kosher salt
- Freshly ground black pepper
- 2 Yukon Gold potatoes, diced
- 1 tablespoon all-purpose flour
- 4 cups Garden Vegetable Stock, or low-sodium store-bought vegetable stock
- 4 ears fresh corn, shucked, kernels cut from cob
- ½ cup quinoa, any color, rinsed well
- ½ cup canned full-fat coconut milk
- 2 tablespoons fresh basil, chopped

Directions:

1. Usea Dutch oven over medium-high heat to heat the olive oil.
2. Add the onion, celery, and red bell pepper together. Season with salt and pepper. Cook for 5 minutes.
3. Add the potatoes. Cook for 3 minutes.
4. Stir in the flour.
5. Pour in the vegetable stock. Add the corn and quinoa. Pour to a boil and reduce to a simmer. Simmer for 15 minutes and wait the potatoes to get soft.
6. Stir in the coconut milk and basil. Season to taste with salt and pepper.

Nutritional Value (Amount per Serving):

- Calories: 388
- Fat: 12.55g
- Carbs: 62.41g
- Protein: 10.59g

Yummy Butternut Goat Cheese Frittata

Prep Time: 10 Minutes
Cook Time: 25 Minutes
Serves: 4

Ingredients:

- 1 medium butternut squash, diced (about 2 cups)
- 2 cups sliced Swiss chard
- 2 tablespoons extra-virgin olive oil
- Celtic sea salt or kosher salt
- Freshly ground black pepper
- 8 large eggs
- 2 ounces soft goat cheese, divided
- ¼ teaspoon red pepper flakes

Directions:

1. Use a 6-inch round cake pan to mix togetherthe squash, Swiss chard, and olive oil. Season with salt and pepper and put the pan in the air fryer's basket. Fry at 370°F for 10 minutes.
2. Remove half the vegetables to another 6-inch round cake pan. Set aside.
3. Crack 4 eggs into the first cake pan and combine well. Break in half the goat cheese and distribute with a pinch of red pepper flakes. Air fry at 370°F for 6 minutes and wait the frittata's center to get puffed and lightly brown.
4. Repeat the steps with the remaining ingredients for other frittatas.

Nutritional Value (Amount per Serving):

- Calories: 230
- Fat: 15.22g
- Carbs: 15.42g
- Protein: 9.62g

CHAPTER 4: CHICKEN

Healthy Roasted Chicken With Carrots Chickpeas

Prep Time: 5 Minutes
Cook Time: 1 Hour
Serves: 4

Ingredients:

- 1 tablespoon extra-virgin olive oil
- 4 bone-in, skin-on chicken thighs
- Celtic sea salt or kosher salt
- Freshly ground black pepper
- 6 carrots, sliced
- 1 teaspoon honey
- 2 cups drained canned chickpeas, or 1½ cups cooked chickpeas
- ½ shallot, finely chopped
- 2 tablespoons fresh parsley, chopped
- ¼ teaspoon dried rosemary, crushed

Directions:

1. Preheat the oven to 375°F.
2. Use a Dutch oven over medium heat for heating the olive oil.
3. Season the chicken with salt and pepper. Cautiously put the chicken, skin-side down in the hot oil. Cook for 8 to 10 minutes and wait it to get golden brown and crisp. Turn the chicken skin-side up.
4. Add the carrots, honey, and chickpeas. Remove the pot to the oven and roast, uncovered, for 40 to 45 minutes. Wait it to get thoroughly cooked.
5. Transfer the chicken from the pot and whisk in the shallot, parsley, and rosemary. Season to taste with salt and pepper. Serve the chicken along with the stew on the side.

Nutritional Value (Amount per Serving):

- Calories: 282
- Fat: 16.24g
- Carbs: 24.94g
- Protein: 10.2g

Easy Sheet Pan Chicken Teriyaki

Prep Time: 10 Minutes
Cook Time: 15 Minutes
Serves: 4

Ingredients:

- ¼ cup low-sodium soy sauce
- 2 tablespoons mirin
- 1 tablespoon honey
- 1 pound boneless, skinless chicken breast, thinly sliced
- 1 cup fresh pineapple chunks
- 2 cups broccoli florets
- 1 red bell pepper, thinly sliced
- 1 cup sugar snap peas, strings removed
- ¼ cup cashews, roughly chopped

Directions:

1. Preheat the oven to 400°F.
2. Use a large bowl to stir the soy sauce, mirin, and honey.
3. Add the chicken and stir to coat.
4. Add the pineapple, broccoli, red bell pepper, as well as peas. Stir to coat. Pour the contents onto a sheet pan. Bake for 15 minutes and wait the chicken to get cooked through.
5. Stir in the cashews.

Nutritional Value (Amount per Serving):

- Calories: 435
- Fat: 19.03g
- Carbs: 50.51g
- Protein: 18.11g

Home-Made Air Fryer Chicken Parmesan With Baby Broccolini

Prep Time: 15 Minutes
Cook Time: 20 Minutes
Serves: 4

Ingredients:

- 1 bunch broccolini (about 4 stems), or 1 cup broccoli florets
- 1 garlic clove, slivered
- Olive oil cooking spray, for preparing the vegetables
- 2 large eggs, beaten
- ½ cup seasoned Italian bread crumbs
- 2 boneless, skinless chicken breasts
- ¼ cup all-purpose flour
- Celtic sea salt or kosher salt
- Freshly ground black pepper
- ½ cup Super Simple Marinara
- 4 ounces provolone cheese, sliced

Directions:

1. Prepare your air fryer's basket and mix together the broccolini and garlic. Spritz the vegetables with cooking spray.
2. Use a shallow bowl prepared in advance to put the beaten eggs and another prepared bowl to put the bread crumbs. Set aside.
3. Cut the chicken breasts in half. Split each half crosswise and do not cut all the way through for forming 4 thin cutlets. Spread the chicken with flour and use salt and pepper for seasoning
4. Dredge each cutlet in egg. Transfer them and coat with bread crumbs. Put the breaded chicken into the air fryer over the broccolini. In line with the size of your fryer basket, you may be required to fry in two batches. Fry at 370°f for 15 minutes.
5. Over the top the chicken with and fry at 370°f for another 5 minutes until the cheese melts and the chicken is cooked through.

Nutritional Value (Amount per Serving):

- Calories: 645
- Fat: 25.15g
- Carbs: 65.36g
- Protein: 37.42g

Fresh Lemon Chicken Tortellini Soup

Prep Time: 10 Minutes
Cook Time: 10 Minutes
Serves: 4

Ingredients:

- 1 tablespoon extra-virgin olive oil
- 1 garlic clove, minced
- 1 leek, white and green parts, thinly sliced
- 2 carrots, sliced
- 6 cups Chicken Stock, or low-sodium store-bought chicken stock
- ½ ounce grated Parmesan cheese
- 9 ounces fresh cheese tortellini
- ½ cup peas, fresh or frozen
- 2 cups fresh baby spinach
- Juice of 1 lemon
- Celtic sea salt or kosher salt
- Freshly ground black pepper

Directions:

1. Use a Dutch oven over medium-high heat for heating the olive oil.
2. Add the garlic, leek, and carrots. Cook for 5 minutes, or until softened.
3. Add the chicken stock and Parmesan. Bring to a boil.
4. Stir in the tortellini. Boil for 5 minutes and wait the tortellini to get cooked through.
5. Stir in the peas, spinach, and lemon juice. Season with salt and pepper and enjoy.

Nutritional Value (Amount per Serving):

- Calories: 376
- Fat: 11.64g
- Carbs: 48.13g
- Protein: 19.65g

Delicious White Pizza With Chicken Red Peppers

Prep Time: 5 Minutes
Cook Time: 10 To 12 Minutes For Each Pizza
Serves: 4

Ingredients:

- 13 ounces pizza dough, at room temperature
- 2 tablespoons extra-virgin olive oil
- 4 garlic cloves, minced
- 1½ cups shredded part-skim mozzarella cheese
- 1 boneless, skinless chicken breast, thinly sliced
- 1 red bell pepper, thinly sliced
- 1 small zucchini, diced

Directions:

1. Separate the pizza dough in half and flatten each half into the shape of an 8-inch round. Cover each round gently with olive oil and spread each with half of the minced garlic. Put ¾ cup of cheese over each round and distribute the chicken, red bell pepper, and zucchini to half of each.
2. Put one round in the air fryer's basket. Fry at 375° F for 10 to 12 minutes and wait the dough to be cooked through.
3. Transfer the pizza from the air fryer and divide it into 4 pieces. Repeat with the second pizza.

Nutritional Value (Amount per Serving):

- Calories: 623
- Fat: 24.85g
- Carbs: 74.38g
- Protein: 24.88g

Yummy Chicken Quinoa Skillet

Prep Time: 15 Minutes
Cook Time: 35 Minutes
Serves: 6

Ingredients:

- 1 tablespoon extra-virgin olive oil
- 1 pound boneless, skinless chicken breast, cut into 1-inch pieces
- 1 small yellow onion, diced
- 2 garlic cloves, minced
- 1 jalapeño pepper, seeded and minced
- 1 (15-ounce) can low-sodium black beans, drained
- 12 ounces no-salt-added chopped tomatoes in purée
- 1 cup water
- 1 tablespoon dried oregano
- 1 cup quinoa, any color (I usually use tricolor), rinsed well
- 6 ounces sharp Cheddar cheese, shredded
- 4 scallions, white and green parts, sliced

Directions:

1. Use a large deep-sided skillet and adjust to medium-high heat for heating the olive oil.
2. Add the chicken. Cook for 7 to 8 minutes with several stirring, or until browned.
3. Add the onion, garlic, and jalapeño. Cook for 4 to 5 minutes and wait it to get softened.
4. Pour together the black beans, tomatoes, and water. Add the oregano. Bring the mixture to a boil.
5. Stir in the quinoa. Cook for another 15 minutes, and wait the quinoa to be well cooked and most of the liquid to get evaporated.
6. Distribute an even layer of cheese to top the dish. Close the skillet and cook for 3 to 4 minutes more to melt the cheese. Top with the sliced scallions before serving.

Nutritional Value (Amount per Serving):

- Calories: 456
- Fat: 18.78g
- Carbs: 50.26g
- Protein: 22.15g

Thai Flavored Basil Chicken

Prep Time: 10 Minutes
Cook Time: 15 Minutes
Serves: 4

Ingredients:

- 1 tablespoon extra-virgin olive oil
- 2 boneless, skinless chicken breasts, thinly sliced
- 1 Thai chile pepper, seeded and minced
- 2 red bell peppers, thinly sliced
- 2 onions, thinly sliced
- 3 tablespoons fish sauce
- 2 tablespoons low-sodium soy sauce
- 1 teaspoon rice vinegar
- 4 cups cauliflower rice
- ¼ cup fresh basil leaves
- 1 lime, quartered

Directions:

1. Use a large skillet and set at high heat to heat the olive oil.
2. Add the chicken. Cook for 3 to 4 minutes and stir from time to time, or until lightly browned.
3. Add the chile pepper, red bell peppers, onions, fish sauce, soy sauce, and vinegar and mix well. Cook for 5 minutes and wait the vegetables to get soft.
4. Add the cauliflower rice. Cook for 3 minutes until softened.
5. Stir in the basil. Serve with the lime wedges for squeezing.

Nutritional Value (Amount per Serving):

- Calories: 929
- Fat: 48.03g
- Carbs: 114.48g
- Protein: 45.35g

Healthy Sheet Pan Jerk Chicken With Potatoes Green Beans

Prep Time: 10 Minutes
Cook Time: 40 Minutes
Serves: 4

Ingredients:

- 4 bone-in chicken thighs, skin removed and discarded
- 1 tablespoon jerk seasoning
- 1 pound baby Yukon Gold potatoes
- 4 carrots, sliced
- 1 pound green beans, trimmed
- 1 tablespoon extra-virgin olive oil
- Celtic sea salt or kosher salt
- Freshly ground black pepper

Directions:

1. Preheat the oven to 450°F.
2. Place a sheet pan with parchment paper. Put the chicken thighs on one side of the sheet pan and bursh each thigh with jerk seasoning gently.
3. Mix together the potatoes, carrots, and green beans and brush on the other side of the pan. Sprinkle with olive oil and season with salt and pepper.
4. Roast for around 35 to 40 minutes and wait the potatoes to get tender and the chicken to get cooked through.

Nutritional Value (Amount per Serving):

- Calories: 579
- Fat: 32.04g
- Carbs: 45.17g
- Protein: 28.58g

Easy Chicken Chorizo Potatoes

Prep Time: 10 Minutes
Cook Time: 30 Minutes
Serves: 4

Ingredients:

- 1 pound small red potatoes, halved
- 1 head broccoli, cut into florets (about 4 cups)
- 2 tablespoons extra-virgin olive oil
- 2 teaspoons paprika
- 1 pound chicken chorizo, cut into rounds
- 3 tablespoons chopped green olives
- 1 tablespoon chopped fresh parsley
- 1 tablespoon chopped fresh oregano leaves

Directions:

1. Preheat the oven to 400°F.
2. Use a large bowl to mix together the potatoes, broccoli, olive oil, and paprika. Blend the vegetables together and pour onto a sheet pan. Distribute the chorizo over the potatoes.
3. Bake for around 20 to 30 minutes and whisk halfway through the baking time, until the potatoes get tender.
4. Transfer from the oven and whisk in the olives, parsley, and oregano.

Nutritional Value (Amount per Serving):

- Calories: 295
- Fat: 7.92g
- Carbs: 26.09g
- Protein: 33.38g

Tasteful Red Curry Ramen

Prep Time: 5 Minutes
Cook Time: 25 Minutes
Serves: 4

Ingredients:

- 6 cups Chicken Stock, or low-sodium store-bought chicken stock
- 1 tablespoon grated peeled fresh ginger
- 1 tablespoon red curry paste
- 1 pound boneless, skinless chicken breast
- 3½ ounces shiitake mushrooms, sliced
- ¼ cup rice vinegar
- 2 tablespoons sesame oil
- 9 ounces ramen noodles, preferably organic
- 2 scallions, white and green parts, sliced (optional)
- 2 Pressure-Cooked Hard-boiled Eggs, halved (optional)

Directions:

1. Use the pressure cooker to mix together the chicken stock, ginger, curry paste, chicken, mushrooms, vinegar, and sesame oil. Close the hood in place and adjust the appliance to High pressure for 20 minutes.
2. When the cook time runs out, manually release the pressure.
3. Cautiously remove the lid and transfer the chicken from the pot.
4. Add the ramen noodles. put it aside and keep it uncovered, for 5 minutes, or until soft.
5. Shred the chicken and transfer it to the pot. Stir to combine.
6. Top the soup with the scallions and eggs (if using).

Nutritional Value (Amount per Serving):

- Calories: 750
- Fat: 32.07g
- Carbs: 83.08g
- Protein: 30.85g

Healthy Crispy Chicken Watermelon Salad

Prep Time: 10 Minutes
Cook Time: 20 Minutes
Serves: 4

Ingredients:

- 2 large eggs, beaten
- ½ cup plain bread crumbs
- 1 pound chicken breast cutlets
- ¼ cup all-purpose flour
- Celtic sea salt or kosher salt
- Freshly ground black pepper
- Olive oil cooking spray, for coating the chicken
- 6 cups arugula
- 2 cups cubed watermelon
- 4 ounces crumbled feta cheese
- ¼ red onion, thinly sliced
- 2 tablespoons chopped walnuts
- ¼ cup balsamic vinegar
- 2 tablespoons extra-virgin olive oil

Directions:

1. Put the beaten eggs in a prepared shallow bowl and place the bread crumbs to another shallow bowl.
2. Distribute the chicken with the flour and season with salt and pepper together. Dredge the chicken in the egg, remove, and cover with the bread crumb coating. Spritz the coated chicken with cooking spray. Put the breaded chicken into the air fryer's basket at 370°F for around 20 minutes, during which time toss halfway through. Cut into bite-size pieces.
3. Use a large salad bowl to mix together the cooked chicken with the arugula, watermelon, cheese, red onion, walnuts, vinegar, and olive oil. Toss to combine. Generously season with salt and pepper.

Nutritional Value (Amount per Serving):

- Calories: 403
- Fat: 17.87g
- Carbs: 30.48g
- Protein: 30.65g

Exotic Balsamic Chicken Mushrooms

Prep Time: 10 Minutes
Cook Time: 15 Minutes
Serves: 4

Ingredients:

- 1 pound chicken breast cutlets
- 2 teaspoons all-purpose flour
- Celtic sea salt or kosher salt
- Freshly ground black pepper
- 1 tablespoon extra-virgin olive oil
- 6 ounces cremini mushrooms, sliced
- ¼ cup Chicken Stock, or low-sodium store-bought chicken stock
- 2 tablespoons balsamic vinegar
- 10 ounces zucchini noodles
- ½ cup cherry tomatoes, halved
- 2 tablespoons fresh parsley, chopped

Directions:

1. Spread the chicken with the flour and use salt and pepper for seasoning.
2. Use a large skillet and adjust at medium-high heat to heat the olive oil.
3. Add the chicken. Cook for around 2 minutes for each side to brown. Transfer the chicken from the skillet and reduce the heat.
4. Add the mushrooms to the skillet. Cook for 5 minutes with several stirring, until deeply browned.
5. Add the chicken stock and vinegar. Bring the mixture to a simmer.
6. Add the zucchini noodles and tomatoes. Return the chicken to the pan. Restart a simmer and cook for another 5 minutes and wait the chicken to be cooked through.
7. Spread with the parsley and use salt and pepper for seasoning, enjoy.

Nutritional Value (Amount per Serving):

- Calories: 363
- Fat: 4.42g
- Carbs: 58.05g
- Protein: 27.34g

Easy Korean Pulled Chicken Lettuce Cups

Prep Time: 10 Minutes
Cook Time: 6 Hours
Serves: 4

Ingredients:

- 1 pound boneless, skinless chicken breasts
- ⅓ cup chili-garlic sauce
- ¼ cup low-sodium soy sauce
- 3 tablespoons honey
- 3 tablespoons rice wine vinegar
- Butter lettuce leaves, for serving
- Quick cucumber pickles, for serving
- Shredded carrots, for serving
- Sliced scallions, white and green parts, for serving

Directions:

1. Prepare a slow cooker for mix together the chicken, chili-garlic sauce, soy sauce, honey, and vinegar. Close the lid and set it to low heat. Cook for 6 hours.
2. Shred the chicken and transfer it to the pot. Keep it for 5 minutes to soak up the sauce.
3. Serve the chicken in lettuce cups, and put pickles, carrots, and scallions over the top.

Nutritional Value (Amount per Serving):

- Calories: 333
- Fat: 8.8g
- Carbs: 48.46g
- Protein: 15.29g

Super-Hot Oven-Roasted Tandoori Chicken Thighs

Prep Time: 10 Minutes
Cook Time: 40 Minutes
Serves: 4

Ingredients:

- ½ cup fat-free plain Greek yogurt
- 1 tablespoon grated peeled fresh ginger
- 1 teaspoon garam masala
- ½ teaspoon ground turmeric
- 1 tablespoon freshly squeezed lemon juice
- Celtic sea salt or kosher salt
- 4 boneless, skinless chicken thighs
- 1 acorn squash, cut into 8 wedges
- 1 small head cauliflower, cut into florets (about 2 cups)
- 4 carrots, sliced
- 1 large tomato, cut into 8 thick wedges
- 1 tablespoon extra-virgin olive oil
- Freshly ground black pepper

Directions:

1. Preheat the oven to 450°F.
2. Use a large bowl to mix together the yogurt, ginger, garam masala, turmeric, lemon juice, as well as a pinch of salt. Add the chicken thighs before turn to coat.
3. Put the acorn squash, cauliflower, carrots, and tomato within a sheet pan. Sprinkle with the olive oil. Use salt and pepper for seasoning. Distribute the vegetables into a single layer. Nestle the chicken into the vegetables.
4. Bake for 25 to 35 minutes, and waith the chicken to get cooked through. You may broil the chicken for 5 minutes more to crisp it as you like.

Nutritional Value (Amount per Serving):

- Calories: 988
- Fat: 30.66g
- Carbs: 127.93g
- Protein: 50.33g

Fresh Lemon Chicken Rice With Artichokes Olives

Prep Time: 5 Minutes
Cook Time: 25 Minutes
Serves: 4

Ingredients:

- 2 tablespoons extra-virgin olive oil
- 1 pound boneless, skinless chicken breasts, diced
- Celtic sea salt or kosher salt
- Freshly ground black pepper
- 2½ cups Chicken Stock, or low-sodium store-bought chicken stock
- 1 onion, diced
- 1 cup uncooked long-grain white rice
- 1 can artichoke heart quarters, drained
- 4 cups fresh spinach
- Juice of 1 lemon
- ½ cup whole pitted Kalamata olives

Directions:

1. Prepare a dutch oven and adjust to medium-high heat for heating the olive oil.
2. Once the oil is hot, add the chicken. Season with salt and pepper. Cook for 3 to 4 minutes with several stirring, to brown.
3. Add the chicken stock, onion, rice, artichokes, spinach, lemon juice, and olives together. Close the lid of the pot and cook for 20 minutes. Wait the liquid to get absorbed and the rice to get cooked through.

Nutritional Value (Amount per Serving):

- Calories: 504
- Fat: 13.68g
- Carbs: 75.08g
- Protein: 19.89g

CHAPTER 5: MEAT

Popular Taco Casserole

Prep Time: 10 Minutes
Cook Time: 25 Minutes
Serves: 4

Ingredients:

- 1 tablespoon extra-virgin olive oil
- 1 onion, chopped
- 2 garlic cloves, minced
- 1 pound lean ground beef
- 2 tablespoons taco seasoning
- 1 zucchini, cut into 1-inch pieces
- 1 (15-ounce) can low-sodium black beans, drained
- 1 cup salsa
- 1 cup shredded Cheddar or Mexican blend cheese
- 1 avocado, sliced (optional)
- 6 ounces corn tortilla chips

Directions:

1. Use a Dutch oven and set it to medium-high heat for heating the olive oil.
2. Add the onion and garlic. Cook for 2 to 3 minutes until softened.
3. Add the ground beef and taco seasoning. Cook for about 5 minutes and stir constantly, until browned.
4. Combine together the zucchini, black beans, and salsa. Mix well. Simmer the mixture for 10 minutes.
5. Top with the cheese. Close the lid of the pot and cook for 3 to 4 minutes until the cheese melts.
6. Top with the avocado (if desired). Serve with the tortilla chips.

Nutritional Value (Amount per Serving):

- Calories: 788
- Fat: 40.15g
- Carbs: 59.32g
- Protein: 47.86g

Jammy Pan-Roasted Pork Chops With Grapes

Prep Time: 10 Minutes
Cook Time: 20 To 25 Minutes
Serves: 4

Ingredients:

- 4 (½-inch-thick) bone-in pork loin chops
- Celtic sea salt or kosher salt
- Freshly ground black pepper
- 1 tablespoon extra-virgin olive oil
- 2 cups Chicken Stock, or low-sodium store-bought chicken stock
- 1 shallot, thinly sliced
- 1 teaspoon chopped fresh rosemary
- ¼ teaspoon dried thyme
- 1 cup quinoa, any color, rinsed well
- 2 cups seedless red grapes, halved

Directions:

1. Preheat the oven to 400°F.
2. Season the pork chops with salt and pepper.
3. Use a large ovenproof skillet and set it to high heat for heating the olive oil.
4. Add the pork chops. Cook for 1 to 2 minutes for each side until browned.
5. Mix together the chicken stock, shallot, rosemary, thyme, quinoa, and grapes and stir well. Remove the skillet to the oven and bake for 15 minutes.
6. Place the pork chops to a plate and cool for a while. If the quinoa needs more time, put the skillet to the oven again for another 5 minutes.

Nutritional Value (Amount per Serving):

- Calories: 599
- Fat: 23.07g
- Carbs: 46.41g
- Protein: 50.04g

Simple Roasted Eggplant With Ground Lamb

Prep Time: 10 Minutes
Cook Time: 50 Minutes
Serves: 6

Ingredients:

- 1 tablespoon extra-virgin olive oil
- 2 garlic cloves, minced
- 1 pound ground lamb
- 2 teaspoons ground coriander
- 1 large (about 1½ pounds) globe eggplant, peeled and cut into 1-inch cubes
- 3 cups grape tomatoes, halved
- 1 tablespoon tomato paste
- ½ cup water
- 2 ounces feta cheese, crumbled
- 2 tablespoons chopped fresh parsley

Directions:

1. Preheat the oven to 400°F.
2. Use a Dutch oven and adjust to medium-high heat to heat the olive oil.
3. Add the garlic. Cook for 1 to 2 minutes until fragrant.
4. Crumble in the lamb and spread in the coriander. Cook for 5 to 7 minutes and stir for several times, until browned.
5. Mix together the eggplant, tomatoes, tomato paste, and water. Combine well. Move the pot to the oven and cook in an uncovered condition, for 30 to 40 minutes until the vegetables get really soft and the liquid gets evaporated.
6. Spread with the cheese and parsley before serving.

Nutritional Value (Amount per Serving):

- Calories: 259
- Fat: 12.71g
- Carbs: 20.34g
- Protein: 18.38g

Easy Sheet Pan Barbecue Baked Ribs

Prep Time: 10 Minutes
Cook Time: 1 Hour
Serves: 4

Ingredients:

- 1½ pounds boneless country-style pork ribs
- 1 tablespoon smoked paprika
- 2 sweet potatoes, cut into ¼-inch sticks
- 1 tablespoon cornstarch
- 1 tablespoon extra-virgin olive oil
- ¼ cup Maple Barbecue Sauce
- 1 pound green beans, trimmed
- Celtic sea salt or kosher salt
- Freshly ground black pepper

Directions:

1. Preheat the oven to 375°F. Place a sheet pan with heavy-duty aluminum foil in a well-arranged way.
   Brush the ribs with the paprika and place them on one side of the prepared sheet pan.
2. Use a medium bowl to fling the sweet potato fries with the cornstarch. Sprinkle them with the olive oil and place the coated sweet potatoes in a line on the other side of the sheet pan. Bake for around 45 minutes and wait the ribs to get tender and get cooked through.
3. Rub the ribs with barbecue sauce. Add the green beans to the pan. Put salt and pepper for seasoning the green beans and sweet potato fries. Bake for around 15 minutes more and wait the vegetables to get soft and the sauce to get nicely caramelized.

Nutritional Value (Amount per Serving):

- Calories: 440
- Fat: 21.65g
- Carbs: 10.44g
- Protein: 52.33g

Yummy Pork Egg Roll In A Bowl

Prep Time: 5 Minutes
Cook Time: 15 Minutes
Serves: 4

Ingredients:

- 1 tablespoon sesame oil
- 4 garlic cloves, minced
- 1 teaspoon grated peeled fresh ginger
- 8 ounces ground pork
- 2 tablespoons low-sodium soy sauce
- 1 tablespoon sambal oelek
- 1 tablespoon rice vinegar
- 6 cups coleslaw mix
- 5 scallions, white and green parts, sliced

Directions:

1. Use a large skillet and adjust to medium-high heat to heat the sesame oil.
2. Add the garlic and ginger. Cook for 2 to 3 minutes until fragrant.
3. Add the ground pork. Cook for 7 to 10 minutes and mash the meat with a spoon, until they get browned and cooked through.
4. Combine together and mix well the soy sauce, sambal oelek, and vinegar. Cook for 1 minute and wait the liquid to get nearly evaporated.
5. Combine well the coleslaw mix. Cook for 2 to 3 minutes until wilted.
6. Stir in the scallions.

Nutritional Value (Amount per Serving):

- Calories: 366
- Fat: 16.08g
- Carbs: 36.95g
- Protein: 18.05g

Delicious Pressure Cooker Bolognese With Spaghetti Squash

Prep Time: 15 Minutes
Cook Time: 15 To 20 Minutes
Serves: 4

Ingredients:

- 4 ounces pancetta, chopped
- 2 celery stalks, chopped
- 2 carrots, grated
- 1 onion, minced
- 1 pound lean ground beef
- 2 cups Super Simple Marinara
- 2 bay leaves
- 1 spaghetti squash, cut crosswise into 4 rings, seeded
- ½ cup half-and-half
- ¼ cup chopped fresh parsley

Directions:

1. Use your pressure cooker and choose Sauté. Put the pancetta into the cooker. Cook for 2 to 3 minutes and stir for several times, or until crisp.
2. Add the celery, carrots, onion, ground beef, marinara, and bay leaves and mix well. Put the squash rings over the sauce. Close the hood in place and set the appliance to High pressure for 12 minutes.
3. When the cook time runs out, manually release the pressure.
4. Cautiously open the lid and transfer the squash rings from the pot. Combine together the half-and-half and parsley. For a thicker sauce, choose Sauté and cook without closing the hood, for 5 minutes more.
5. To serve, spoon the sauce over the squash rings.

Nutritional Value (Amount per Serving):

- Calories: 386
- Fat: 17.44g
- Carbs: 16.84g
- Protein: 39.76g

Quintessential Slow Cooker Beef Stew

Prep Time: 15 Minutes
Cook Time: 8 Hours
Serves: 6

Ingredients:

- 2 pounds chuck roast, trimmed and cut into 1-inch pieces
- ¼ cup white whole-wheat flour
- Celtic sea salt or kosher salt
- Freshly ground black pepper
- 4 garlic cloves, smashed
- 6 carrots, sliced
- 3 red potatoes, diced
- 1 onion, chopped
- 2 cups low-sodium beef stock, or Garden Vegetable Stock, or low-sodium store-bought vegetable stock
- ½ cup red wine (optional)
- 2 tablespoons tomato paste
- ¼ cup fresh parsley, chopped

Directions:

1. Prepare a slow cooker to mix together the beef and flour. Whisk to coat. Generously season with salt and pepper.
2. Add the garlic, carrots, potatoes, onion, stock, red wine (if using), and tomato paste together. Close the lid of the appliance and set at low heat. Cook for 8 hours, or until the beef is very tender.
3. Stir in the parsley and try with the seasoning as you like.

Nutritional Value (Amount per Serving):

- Calories: 504
- Fat: 15.14g
- Carbs: 45.21g
- Protein: 48.63g

Goulash Soup

Prep Time: 10 Minutes
Cook Time: 40 Minutes
Serves: 4

Ingredients:

- 2 tablespoons extra-virgin olive oil
- 1 pound boneless chuck roast, cut into ½-inch pieces
- Celtic sea salt or kosher salt
- Freshly ground black pepper
- 4 garlic cloves, minced
- 4 cups Chicken Stock, or low-sodium store-bought chicken stock
- 2 carrots, sliced
- 2 celery stalks, thinly sliced
- 1 onion, diced
- 1 red bell pepper, chopped
- ¼ cup sweet Hungarian paprika
- 1 bay leaf
- 2 tablespoons red wine vinegar

Directions:

1. Prepare a pressure cooker and select sauté. Pour in the olive oil to heat.
2. Add the beef. Cook for 3 to 4 minutes and stir for several times, until browned. Season with salt and pepper.
3. Stir in the garlic. Cook for 1 minute. Add and mix together the chicken stock, carrots, celery, onion, red bell pepper, paprika, and bay leaf. Close the hood in place and adjust the cooker to high pressure for 35 minutes.
4. Once the cook time runs out, make the pressure release naturally for 10 minutes; manually release any remaining pressure.
5. Cautiously open the lid and remove and discard the bay leaf. Stir in the vinegar.

Nutritional Value (Amount per Serving):

- Calories: 363
- Fat: 16.47g
- Carbs: 16.93g
- Protein: 38.06g

Classic Stuffed Peppers

Prep Time: 10 Minutes
Cook Time: 20 Minutes
Serves: 4

Ingredients:

- 2 cups cauliflower rice
- 1 pound lean ground beef
- 1 cup Super Simple Marinara
- ¼ cup grated Parmesan cheese
- ¼ cup fresh parsley, chopped
- 1 teaspoon Italian seasoning
- ½ teaspoon garlic powder
- Celtic sea salt or kosher salt
- Freshly ground black pepper
- 4 red bell peppers, tops removed, seeded, and ribbed
- Olive oil cooking spray, for spritzing
- ¼ cup shredded part-skim mozzarella cheese, divided

Directions:

1. Use a large bowl to mix together the cauliflower rice, ground beef, marinara, Parmesan, parsley, Italian seasoning, and garlic powder. Use salt and pepper for seasoning. Stuff the filling into the peppers. Sprinkle the peppers and stuffing with cooking spray.
2. Put the stuffed peppers in the prepared air fryer's basket and select fry model at 350°F for 15 to 18 minutes, and wait the beef to get cooked through (the temperature should be at least 160°F in line with a meat thermometer).
3. Pour 1 tablespoon of mozzarella cheese over the top of each pepper and make second fry for another 1 to 2 minutes to melt the cheese.

Nutritional Value (Amount per Serving):

- Calories: 486
- Fat: 28.26g
- Carbs: 32.16g
- Protein: 41.92g

Corned Beef Reuben Chowder

Prep Time: 15 Minutes
Cook Time: 30 Minutes
Serves: 6

Ingredients:

- 1 tablespoon unsalted butter
- 1 onion, chopped
- 4 ounces uncured corned beef, thickly sliced and chopped
- 2 russet potatoes, diced
- 2 tablespoons all-purpose flour
- 4 cups Chicken Stock, or low-sodium store-bought chicken stock
- 1 cup sauerkraut, drained
- ¼ cup sour cream
- 1 cup shredded Swiss cheese
- 4 scallions, white and green parts, chopped

Directions:

1. Use a Dutch oven and adjust to medium heat to melt the butter.
2. Add the onion. Cook for 2 to 3 minutes until softened.
3. Add the corned beef. Cook for 5 minutes and wait the edges to begin to curl.
4. Stir in the potatoes. Cook for 2 minutes. Distribute in the flour and mix well to combine.
5. Whisk in the chicken stock and sauerkraut. Put the chowder to a simmer. Simmer for 15 minutes and wait the potatoes to get cooked through. Remove from the heat.
6. Stir in the sour cream and cheese gently and lightly. Top with the scallions before serving.

Nutritional Value (Amount per Serving):

- Calories: 313
- Fat: 11.63g
- Carbs: 35.29g
- Protein: 17.77g

Easy Baked Sausage Risotto

Prep Time: 10 Minutes
Cook Time: 30 Minutes
Serves: 4

Ingredients:

- 1 tablespoon extra-virgin olive oil
- 8 ounces Italian-style turkey sausage, crumbled
- 1 onion, diced
- 3 garlic cloves, minced
- ¾ cup Arborio rice
- 2½ cups Chicken Stock, or low-sodium store-bought chicken stock
- ¼ cup grated Parmesan cheese
- 3 cups chopped kale
- Celtic sea salt or kosher salt
- Freshly ground black pepper

Directions:

1. Preheat the oven to 425°F.
2. Use a Dutch oven and adjust to medium-high heat to heat the olive oil.
3. Add the sausage. Cook for 4 to 5 minutes until browned.
4. Stir in the onion and garlic. Cook for 1 to 2 minutes to soften.
5. Mix together the rice, chicken stock, cheese, and kale. Close the lid of the pot and transfer it to the oven. Bake for 20 minutes and wait the liquid to get absorbed and the rice to get tender and creamy. Season to taste with salt and pepper.

Nutritional Value (Amount per Serving):

- Calories: 274
- Fat: 14.82g
- Carbs: 24.16g
- Protein: 18.08g

Childhood Flavor Sweet Sour Pork Stir-Fry

Prep Time: 10 Minutes
Cook Time: 15 Minutes
Serves: 4

Ingredients:

- 1 tablespoon extra-virgin olive oil
- 1 tablespoon grated peeled fresh ginger
- 1 pound pork loin, cut into bite-size pieces
- 1 cup fresh pineapple chunks, cut into bite-size pieces
- 1 green bell pepper, cut into bite-size pieces
- 4 ounces green beans, trimmed
- ¼ cup apple cider vinegar
- 2 tablespoons packed light brown sugar
- 2 tablespoons honey
- 2 tablespoons low-sodium soy sauce
- 2 tablespoons cornstarch

Directions:

1. Use a large skillet and setcat medium-high heat to heat the olive oil.
2. Add the ginger. Cook for 1 to 2 minutes until fragrant.
3. Add the pork. Cook for 3 to 4 minutes and stir for several times, until browned but not cooked through.
4. Mix together the pineapple, green bell pepper, green beans, vinegar, brown sugar, honey, soy sauce, and cornstarch. Place the mixture to a simmer and cook for 5 to 7 minutes until the vegetables get soft and the pork get cooked through.

Nutritional Value (Amount per Serving):

- Calories: 397
- Fat: 15.37g
- Carbs: 33.64g
- Protein: 31.13g

Easy Air-Fried Lamb Meat Pies

Prep Time: 10 Minutes
Cook Time: 15 Minutes
Serves: 4

Ingredients:

- 8 ounces lamb stew meat, finely chopped
- ½ turnip, finely diced
- 1 carrot, finely diced
- 1 shallot, minced
- 2 tablespoons chopped fresh parsley
- ½ teaspoon dried thyme
- Celtic sea salt or kosher salt
- Freshly ground black pepper
- 1 refrigerated piecrust
- 1 large egg yolk
- 1 tablespoon water

Directions:

1. Use a medium bowl to mix together the lamb, turnip, carrot, shallot, parsley, and thyme. Generously season with salt and pepper.
2. Divide the piecrust into 4 equal pieces. Use spoon to take the filling into the center of each piece of crust. Fold the dough on top of the filling to create a wedge shape. Press the edges tightly for better sealing the filling inside.
3. In the bowl used for the filling, stir in the egg yolk and water and mix well. Rub the egg wash on the pastry. Put the pies in the prepared air fryer's basket and set fry model at 350°F for 12 minutes, or until golden brown and flaky.
4. Make the meat pies cool for 10 minutes before serving, as the inside would be very hot.

Nutritional Value (Amount per Serving):

- Calories: 125
- Fat: 6.4g
- Carbs: 7.47g
- Protein: 9.08g

Yummy Barbecue Meatloaf Mashed Potatoes

Prep Time: 10 Minutes
Cook Time: 30 Minutes
Serves: 4

Ingredients:

- Olive oil cooking spray
- 1 pound small red potatoes, quartered
- ¼ cup water
- 12 ounces lean ground beef
- 1 large egg
- ¼ cup plain bread crumbs
- 1 teaspoon steak seasoning
- ½ teaspoon onion powder
- ¼ cup Maple Barbecue Sauce, or your favorite store-bought barbecue sauce
- 12 ounces green beans, trimmed
- Celtic sea salt or kosher salt
- Freshly ground black pepper
- 1 tablespoon unsalted butter
- ½ cup fat-free plain Greek yogurt

Directions:

1. Preheat the oven to 425°F.
2. Put cooking spray to sprinkle a 12-inch-long piece of foil. Put the potatoes over the foil and spread them with the water. Wrap the foil around the potatoes and seal them tightly before putting the packet on a sheet pan.
3. Use a large bowl to mix together the ground beef, egg, bread crumbs, steak seasoning, and onion powder. Make the meat blend in an 8-by-4-inch loaf over the other side of the sheet pan. Distribute the barbecue sauce across the meatloaf. Bake for 15 minutes.
4. Add the green beans to the pan. Sprinkle with cooking spray and use salt and pepper for seasoning. Bake for 15 minutes more.

5.Cautiously unfold the potatoes and make a bowl out of the foil. Combine the butter and yogurt together and put into the potatoes. Take a potato masher or heavy wooden spoon to grind the potatoes. Season to taste with salt and pepper.

Nutritional Value (Amount per Serving):

- Calories: 395
- Fat: 13.63g
- Carbs: 39.43g
- Protein: 28.45g

Simple Pork Green Bean Stir-Fry

Prep Time: 10 Minutes
Cook Time: 15 Minutes
Serves: 6

Ingredients:

- ¼ cup Chicken Stock, or low-sodium store-bought chicken stock
- 2 tablespoons low-sodium soy sauce
- 1 tablespoon rice vinegar
- 1 to 2 tablespoons sambal oelek (chili paste)
- 2 teaspoons sesame oil
- 1 tablespoon extra-virgin olive oil
- 4 large garlic cloves, minced
- 1 tablespoon grated peeled fresh ginger
- 8 ounces lean ground pork
- 2 cups cauliflower rice
- 8 ounces green beans, trimmed

Directions:

1. Prepare a small bowl to mix together the chicken stock, soy sauce, vinegar, sambal oelek, and sesame oil. Set aside.
2. Use a large skillet and adjust to medium-high heat for heating the olive oil.
3. Add the garlic and ginger. Cook for 2 to 3 minutes and wait they to get soften.
4. Add the ground pork. Cook for 5 minutes and stir for several times, or until nearly cooked through.
5. Whisk in the cauliflower rice, green beans, and sauce. Bring to a simmer. Cook for 5 to 7 minutes and wait the pork to get cooked through.

Nutritional Value (Amount per Serving):

- Calories: 215
- Fat: 12.73g
- Carbs: 23.4g
- Protein: 14.66g

CHAPTER 6: SEAFOOD

Simple Red Curry Salmon With Vegetables

Prep Time: 10 Minutes
Cook Time: 10 Minutes
Serves: 4

Ingredients:

- 1 tablespoon red curry paste
- 1 tablespoon full-fat coconut milk
- 1 teaspoon freshly squeezed lime juice
- 4 (5-ounce) salmon fillets
- 1 pound asparagus, woody ends trimmed
- 1 red bell pepper, sliced
- Celtic sea salt or kosher salt
- Freshly ground black pepper
- Olive oil cooking spray, for preparing the vegetables

Directions:

1. Use a small bowl to combine well the curry paste, coconut milk, and lime juice to form a smooth paste. Distribute the curry paste over the salmon skin.
2. Prepare the air fryer's basket and mix together the asparagus and red bell pepper. Season with salt and pepper. Sprinkle the vegetables with cooking spray.
3. Put the salmon, skin-side up, over the vegetables. Select fry model at 375°f for 5 to 8 minutes and wait the salmon to get cooked through and flake easily with a fork.

Nutritional Value (Amount per Serving):

- Calories: 86
- Fat: 3.42g
- Carbs: 6.67g
- Protein: 8.95g

15-Minute Mussels Provençal

Prep Time: 10 Minutes
Cook Time: 15 Minutes
Serves: 4

Ingredients:

- 2 tablespoons extra-virgin olive oil
- 1 fennel bulb, cored, white part thinly sliced
- 1 pint mushrooms, sliced
- 4 garlic cloves, minced
- 1 shallot, minced
- 1 tomato, diced
- 1 green bell pepper, sliced
- 2 tablespoons water
- 3 pounds mussels, scrubbed well
- 1 whole-grain baguette (optional)

Directions:

1. Use a Dutch oven and adjust to medium-high heat to heat the olive oil.
2. Add the fennel, mushrooms, garlic, and shallot together. Cook for around 4 to 5 minutes, and stir for several times until softened.
3. Whisk in the tomato, green bell pepper, and water. Cook for another 4 to 5 minutes, and stir for several times, or wait the tomato to break down into a sauce.
4. Add the mussels. Close the lid of the pot and cook for around 5 to 7 minutes, or until the mussels open. Remove any mussels that do not open.
5. Serve with the baguette for sopping (if using).

Nutritional Value (Amount per Serving):

- Calories: 746
- Fat: 13.69g
- Carbs: 103.56g
- Protein: 57.17g

Tasteful Pressure Cooker Cioppino

Prep Time: 5 Minutes
Cook Time: 7 Minutes
Serves: 4

Ingredients:

- 1 tablespoon extra-virgin olive oil
- 2 celery stalks, minced
- 1 onion, minced
- 1 green bell pepper, minced
- 2 garlic cloves, thinly sliced
- 4 cups Super Simple Marinara
- 1¼ cups low-sodium fish stock
- 1 teaspoon dried oregano
- Generous pinch saffron threads
- 1 pound frozen medium shrimp
- 1 pound frozen scallops
- 2 tablespoons chopped fresh parsley
- Celtic sea salt or kosher salt
- Freshly ground black pepper

Directions:

1. Use your pressure cooker and adjust to Sauté. Pour in the olive oil to heat.
2. Add the celery, onion, green bell pepper, and garlic together. Cook for 3 to 4 minutes to soften.
3. Mix together and toss well the marinara, fish stock, oregano, and saffron threads. Add the shrimp and scallops. Close the hood in place and adjust the cooker at High pressure for 3 minutes.
4. Once the cook time runs out, make the pressure release naturally for 10 minutes before manually releasing any remaining pressure.
5. Cautiously open the lid and put parsley over the cioppino. Season to taste with salt and pepper.

Nutritional Value (Amount per Serving):

- Calories: 408
- Fat: 10.12g
- Carbs: 69.89g
- Protein: 14.88g

Yummy Shrimp Sausage Paella

Prep Time: 5 Minutes
Cook Time: 35 Minutes
Serves: 4

Ingredients:

- 1 tablespoon extra-virgin olive oil
- 1 onion, chopped
- 1 red bell pepper, chopped
- 4 ounces chicken chorizo, diced
- 2 cups long-grain white rice
- 5 cups Chicken Stock, or low-sodium store-bought chicken stock
- Generous pinch saffron threads
- 1 pound fresh shrimp, peeled and deveined
- 1 cup peas, fresh or frozen
- ¼ cup fresh parsley
- Juice of 1 lemon
- Celtic sea salt or kosher salt

Directions:

1. Prepare a large skillet and adjust to medium heat to heat the olive oil.
2. Once the oil gets hot, add the onion and red bell pepper together. Sauté for 3 to 5 minutes to soften.
3. Add the chorizo. Cook for another 5 minutes until it gets brown.
4. Whisk and combine well the rice, chicken stock, and saffron threads. Cook for 20 minutes, and wait most of the stock to get absorbed and the rice to get soft.
5. Add the shrimp and peas. Cook for 5 minutes, and wait the shrimp to turn into opaque and it gets cooked through.
6. Stir in the parsley and lemon juice. Season to taste with salt.

Nutritional Value (Amount per Serving):

- Calories: 650
- Fat: 8.62g
- Carbs:94.8 g
- Protein: 44.75g

Exquisite Manhattan Clam Chowder

Prep Time: 15 Minutes
Cook Time: 25 Minutes
Serves: 4

Ingredients:

- 4 sugar-free bacon slices, chopped
- 1 onion, diced
- 4 garlic cloves, minced
- 2 celery stalks, diced
- 2 carrots, diced
- 1 teaspoon dried oregano
- 1 (15-ounce) can diced fire-roasted tomatoes
- 2 red potatoes, diced
- 1 cup Chicken Stock, or low-sodium store-bought chicken stock
- 1 (10-ounce) can baby clams
- Juice of 1 lemon
- Celtic sea salt or kosher salt
- Freshly ground black pepper

Directions:

1. Use a Dutch oven and adjust to high heat for frying the bacon for 5 minutes, or until crispy. Turn the heat to low.
2. Add the onion, garlic, celery, carrots, and oregano and mix well. Cook for 5 minutes, stir for several times, until the vegetables get soften.
3. Mix together the tomatoes, potatoes, chicken stock, and clams and put them into it. Bring the chowder to a simmer. Cook for around 15 minutes before the potatoes and carrots turn to soft.
4. Transfer from the heat and whisk in the lemon juice. Season to taste with salt and pepper.

Nutritional Value (Amount per Serving):

- Calories: 213
- Fat: 1.4g
- Carbs: 45.5g
- Protein: 6.71g

Casual Sheet Pan Lemon-Herb Tuna With Gnocchi

Prep Time: 10 Minutes
Cook Time: 25 Minutes
Serves: 4

Ingredients:

- 4 (4-ounce) tuna steaks
- ½ teaspoon dried oregano
- ½ teaspoon dried thyme
- 1 lemon, sliced
- 1 pound dry gnocchi
- 1 zucchini, diced
- 1 tablespoon extra-virgin olive oil
- Celtic sea salt or kosher salt
- Freshly ground black pepper

Directions:

1. Preheat the oven to 450°F.
2. Put the tuna steaks on one side of a sheet pan and brush each with the oregano and thyme. Arrange 1 lemon slice over each tuna steak.
3. Sprinkle the gnocchi and zucchini across the rest of the pan, mash any pieces of gnocchi that are tightly connected. Spread with the olive oil and blend to coat. Season with salt and pepper.
4. Bake for around 20 to 25 minutes and wait the gnocchi to get soft and the tuna to get cooked as you like.

Nutritional Value (Amount per Serving):

- Calories: 787
- Fat: 34.69g
- Carbs: 75.74g
- Protein: 47.65g

Perfect Pressure Cooker Shrimp Boil

Prep Time: 5 Minutes
Cook Time: 1 Minute
Serves: 4

Ingredients:

- 1 pound baby red potatoes, halved
- 2 andouille links, sliced
- 1 cup Chicken Stock, or low-sodium store-bought chicken stock
- 4 ears fresh corn, shucked and halved crosswise
- 1 tablespoon reduced-sodium Old Bay seasoning
- 1 tablespoon hot sauce
- 1 pound frozen (large) peel-and-eat shrimp
- 1 tablespoon unsalted butter
- ¼ cup fresh parsley leaves
- 1 lemon, cut into wedges

Directions:

1. Use the pressure cooker to mix together the potatoes, sausage, chicken stock, corn, seasoning, hot sauce, and shrimp. Close the hood in place and adjust the cooker to High pressure for 1 minute.
2. Once the cook time runs out, make the pressure release naturally for 10 minutes before manually releasing any remaining pressure.
3. Cautiously open the hood and stir in the butter and parsley. Serve with the lemon wedges for squeezing.

Nutritional Value (Amount per Serving):

- Calories: 500
- Fat: 18.2g
- Carbs: 73.84g
- Protein: 17.53g

Yummy Oven-Blackened Tilapia

Prep Time: 10 Minutes
Cook Time: 15 Minutes
Serves: 4

Ingredients:

- 2 tablespoons paprika
- 1 teaspoon Celtic sea salt or kosher salt, plus more for seasoning
- 1 teaspoon onion powder
- 1 teaspoon garlic powder
- 1 teaspoon dried parsley
- ¼ teaspoon cayenne pepper
- 4 (4-ounce) tilapia fillets
- Olive oil cooking spray, for preparing the fish
- 1 pound zucchini noodles
- 1 tablespoon extra-virgin olive oil
- Freshly ground black pepper
- 1 lemon, cut into wedges

Directions:

1. Preheat the oven to 400°F.
2. Prepare a small bowl to combine well the paprika, salt, onion powder, garlic powder, parsley, and cayenne. Put the tilapia fillets on one side of a sheet pan and brush with cooking spray. Cover each with the blackening rub.
3. Distribute the zucchini noodles on the other side of the pan. Sprinkle with the olive oil.
4. Bake for around 12 to 15 minutes and wait the tilapia to get cooked thoroughly (it would turn into opaque and flake easily with a fork).
5. Season the zucchini noodles with salt and pepper properly. Serve the tilapia over the zucchini, and put the lemon wedges on the side for squeezing.

Nutritional Value (Amount per Serving):

- Calories: 292
- Fat: 4.29g
- Carbs: 35.04g
- Protein: 28.65g

CHAPTER 7: DESSERTS

Leisure-Time Blueberry Crisp

Prep Time: 10 Minutes
Cook Time: 45 Minutes To 1 Hour
Serves: 6

Ingredients:

- 2 pints fresh blueberries
- 2 tablespoons honey
- 1 tablespoon cornstarch
- 1 teaspoon ground cinnamon
- Juice of 1 lemon
- ⅓ cup all-purpose flour
- ⅓ cup packed light brown sugar
- ¼ cup rolled oats
- ½ teaspoon baking powder
- 2 tablespoons coconut oil

Directions:

1. Preheat the oven to 375°F.
2. Prepare a dutch oven to mix together the blueberries, honey, cornstarch, cinnamon, and lemon juice.
3. Use a medium bowl to blend well the flour, brown sugar, oats, baking powder, and coconut oil until they are well crumbly. Distribute the crumble over the berries.
4. Bake for around 45 minutes to 1 hour and waith the berries to get bubbling and the crumble crisp and golden brown. Put it aside for cooling for 15 minutes before serving.

Nutritional Value (Amount per Serving):

- Calories: 243
- Fat: 5.68g
- Carbs: 50.08g
- Protein: 2.59g

Sweet Pumpkin Pie Rice Pudding

Prep Time: 5 Minutes
Cook Time: 25 Minutes
Serves: 6

Ingredients:

- ½ cup long-grain white rice
- 2 cups water
- 1 cup fat-free evaporated milk
- ½ cup pumpkin purée
- ¼ cup sugar
- ¼ cup maple syrup
- 1 teaspoon pumpkin pie spice
- ½ teaspoon Celtic sea salt or kosher salt

Directions:

1. Prepare a dutch oven and adjust to high heat. Mix together the rice and water. Cook for about 15 minutes and wait the rice to get nearly cooked and the water to be evaporated.
2. Whisk in the milk, pumpkin purée, sugar, maple syrup, pumpkin pie spice, and salt. Cook for around 7 to 10 minutes with continuous stirring, until thickened.
3. Serve chilled.

Nutritional Value (Amount per Serving):

- Calories: 178
- Fat: 5.04g
- Carbs: 28.93g
- Protein: 5.45g

Lightly Sweet Peach Cobbler

Prep Time: 15 Minutes
Cook Time: 4 Hours
Serves: 6

Ingredients:

- Nonstick cooking spray, for preparing the slow cooker
- 5 fresh peaches, peeled and sliced
- ¼ cup honey
- 1 tablespoon cornstarch
- ½ teaspoon ground cinnamon
- ½ teaspoon ground ginger
- 1¼ cups all-purpose flour
- 3 tablespoons sugar
- 1 teaspoon baking powder
- Pinch Celtic sea salt or kosher salt
- 4 tablespoons cold unsalted butter
- ¾ cup milk, or nondairy milk

Directions:

1. Put cooking spray to cover the slow cooker. Mix together the peaches, honey, cornstarch, cinnamon, and ginger. Mix well.
2. Prepare a medium bowl to put the flour, sugar, baking powder, and salt. Grate in the butter. Lightly combine them to make a crumbly mixture. Stir in the milk for making a wet dough. Drop a big piece of dough over the peaches.
3. Top the cooker with a paper towel for trapping condensation, and close the hood on the top of the paper towel. Adjust the cooker to high heat. Cook for 4 hours and wait the fruit to get soft and the biscuits to get fluffy.

Nutritional Value (Amount per Serving):

- Calories: 387
- Fat: 6.63g
- Carbs: 82.4g
- Protein: 5.01g

Light And Moist Chocolate Zucchini Cake

Prep Time: 10 Minutes
Cook Time: 25 Minutes
Serves: 6

Ingredients:

- 8 tablespoons (1 stick) unsalted butter
- ⅓ cup sugar
- ⅓ cup maple syrup
- 1 teaspoon vanilla extract
- ¼ cup unsweetened cocoa powder
- 2 large eggs
- ½ cup white whole-wheat flour
- ½ cup almond flour
- ½ teaspoon baking powder
- ¼ teaspoon Celtic sea salt or kosher salt
- 2 cups finely shredded zucchini

Directions:

1. Preheat the oven to 350°F.
2. Prepare a 9-inch skillet and set it to medium heat for melting the butter. Transfer the skillet from the heat and mix together the sugar, maple syrup, vanilla, and cocoa powder. Put aside for cooling of about 5 minutes.
3. Whisk in the eggs.
4. Whisk in the whole-wheat and almond flours, baking powder, and salt. Fold in the zucchini.
5. Bake for around 18 to 20 minutes and wait the center to be set and a toothpick piercing into the middle of the cake to be clean as it comes out.
6. Put aside and make the cake cool completely. Turn the cake out onto a cutting board and divide it into 6 chunks to serve.

Nutritional Value (Amount per Serving):

- Calories: 233
- Fat: 12.54g
- Carbs: 28.83g
- Protein: 3.72g

Buttery Cranberry Oatmeal Bars

Prep Time: 10 Minutes
Cook Time: 25 Minutes
Serves: 6

Ingredients:

- ½ cup coconut oil
- ¾ cup maple syrup
- 1 teaspoon vanilla extract
- 1½ cups rolled oats
- 1½ cups white whole-wheat flour
- 1 teaspoon Celtic sea salt
- ½ teaspoon ground cinnamon
- ½ teaspoon baking soda
- 3 cups fresh cranberries, chopped
- 1 tablespoon sugar
- 2 tablespoons sliced almonds

Directions:

1. Preheat the oven to 350°F.
2. Use a large bowl to mix together and stir in the coconut oil and maple syrup until smooth. Stir in the vanilla.
3. Gently blend the oats, flour, salt, cinnamon, and baking soda well to make a crumbly dough. Press half the dough onto one side of a sheet pan, thus to make a layer about ½ inch thick.
4. Sprinkle the chopped cranberries on the top of the dough and cover with the sugar.
5. Crumble the remaining dough over the berries. Sprinkle the top with the almonds.
6. Bake for around 22 to 25 minutes until it gets light golden brown.
7. Transfer from the oven and put it aside for cooling completely. Cut into 6 bars to serve.

Nutritional Value (Amount per Serving):

- Calories: 509
- Fat: 20.48g
- Carbs: 84.59g
- Protein: 7.4g

Sweet Banana Donut Holes

Prep Time: 10 Minutes
Cook Time: 8 Minutes
Serves: 4

Ingredients:

- 1 cup white whole-wheat flour
- 2 tablespoons granulated sugar
- ¼ teaspoon baking powder
- Dash Celtic sea salt or kosher salt
- 2 ripe bananas, mashed
- 2 tablespoons milk, or nondairy milk
- ¼ teaspoon vanilla extract
- Nonstick cooking spray
- 1 tablespoon cinnamon sugar

Directions:

1. Put a large bowl to mix together the flour, granulated sugar, baking powder, and salt.
2. Combine together the bananas, milk, and vanilla, mix well until it turns to be a thick, smooth dough.
3. Shower your air fryer's basket with cooking spray. Place rounded tablespoons of dough into the basket and ensure the spaces between each donut for the air to circulate. Spread the donut holes with cooking spray and set fry model at 360°F for 6 to 8 minutes until it gets golden brown and crisp.
4. Distribute the donuts with the cinnamon sugar. Put it aside to cool for 5 minutes before serving, as it will be very hot inside.

Nutritional Value (Amount per Serving):

- Calories: 206
- Fat: 3.53g
- Carbs: 40.35g
- Protein: 3.99g

Easy Apple Mixed Berry Galette

Prep Time: 10 Minutes
Cook Time: 30 Minutes
Serves: 8

Ingredients:

- Nonstick cooking spray, for preparing the sheet pan
- 1 refrigerated piecrust
- 1 tablespoon flaxseed meal
- 1 apple, cored and thinly sliced
- 1 cup fresh blueberries
- 1 cup sliced fresh strawberries
- 2 tablespoons sugar
- 1 tablespoon lemon zest
- ¼ teaspoon Celtic sea salt or kosher salt
- 1 large egg
- 1 tablespoon water

Directions:

1. Preheat the oven to 450°F. Coat a sheet pan with cooking spray.
2. Put the piecrust on the center of the prepared sheet pan. Spread it with the flaxseed meal.
3. Prepare a small bowl to mix well the apple, blueberries, strawberries, sugar, lemon zest, and salt. Place the filling into the center of the piecrust and ensure 1-inch border around the edge. Close the edge of the dough up and put it on the top of the fruit.
4. In the bowl for the filling, stir the egg and water together. Rub the egg wash over the crust.
5. Bake the galette for around 25 to 30 minutes and wait the crust to get golden brown and the filling to get bubbly. Let cool before serving.

Nutritional Value (Amount per Serving):

- Calories: 72
- Fat: 1.35g
- Carbs: 15.04g
- Protein: 1.15g

Super Soft Oatmeal–Chocolate Chip Cookies

Prep Time: 15 Minutes
Cook Time: 15 Minutes
Serves: 6

Ingredients:

- 2 tablespoons coconut oil
- 2 tablespoons packed light brown sugar
- 1 large egg white
- ¼ teaspoon vanilla extract
- ¼ cup white whole-wheat flour
- ½ teaspoon baking powder
- Pinch Celtic sea salt or kosher salt
- ¾ cup rolled oats
- ¼ cup dark chocolate chips
- ¼ cup unsweetened shredded coconut

Directions:

1. Preheat the oven to 350°F. Place a sheet pan with parchment paper.
2. Use a large bowl to mix well the coconut oil and brown sugar until they are creamed together.
3. Whisk in the egg white and vanilla.
4. Combine well the flour, baking powder, and salt to make a thin dough. Stir in the oats, chocolate chips, and coconut. Drop dozens of tablespoons of dough onto your sheet pan.
5. Bake for around 14 to 16 minutes and waith the centers to gey set and the edges to turn into golden brown. Put the cookies aside and get cool for at least 5 minutes before transferring from the sheet pan.

Nutritional Value (Amount per Serving):

- Calories: 207
- Fat: 11.34g
- Carbs: 26.51g
- Protein: 4.43g

CHAPTER 8: SNACKS & SIDES

Crispy Salt Visnegar Chickpeas

Prep Time: 5 Minutes
Cook Time: 15 Minutes
Serves: 6

Ingredients:

- 1 (15-ounce) can low-sodium chickpeas, drained
- 1 tablespoon malt vinegar or distilled white vinegar
- ½ teaspoon extra-virgin olive oil
- ½ teaspoon Celtic sea salt

Directions:

1. Use a small bowl to whisk together the chickpeas, vinegar, olive oil, and salt. Combine well. Remove the chickpeas to the preapred air fryer's basket and select fry model at 370°F for 15 minutes, tossing the basket in-between the cooking time.
2. Make the chickpeas cool in a single layer. The chickpeas are expected to get crispy as they cool.
3. To store, you need to drain them. To put them into refrigerator, they should be covered, for 3 to 5 days, or freeze for up to 3 months.

Nutritional Value (Amount per Serving):

- Calories: 68
- Fat: 1.62g
- Carbs: 10.1g
- Protein: 3.68g

Broiling Baba Ghanoush

Prep Time: 10 Minutes
Cook Time: 10 Minutes
Serves: 6

Ingredients:

- 1 large (about 1 pound) globe eggplant, cut into ½-inch-thick rounds
- 2 tablespoons tahini
- 2 garlic cloves, peeled
- Juice of 1 lemon
- ¼ cup fresh cilantro or parsley
- 1 teaspoon Celtic sea salt
- Pinch ground cumin
- 1 teaspoon extra-virgin olive oil

Directions:

1. Preheat the broiler.
2. Put the eggplant rounds on a sheet pan. Broil for 10 minutes and wait them to get soft and golden brown. Use a spoon to take the eggplant into a blender, discarding the skin.
3. Combine together the tahini, garlic, lemon juice, cilantro, salt, and cumin and add into it. Blend into a thick paste. Scrape the dip into a bowl and distribute with the olive oil. Close the lid and put into refrigerator until ready to serve. The baba ghanoush will keep, refrigerated, for 3 to 5 days.

Nutritional Value (Amount per Serving):

- Calories: 61
- Fat: 3.29g
- Carbs: 7.63g
- Protein: 1.98g

Fast Pickles

Prep Time: 5 Minutes
Cook Time: 5 Minutes
Serves: 6

Ingredients:

- 1 cup thinly sliced vegetable of choice
- 2 garlic cloves, smashed
- ½ cup apple cider vinegar
- 1 teaspoon honey
- Pinch Celtic sea salt or kosher salt

Directions:

1. Prepare the vegetables and garlic in a heat-proof container.
2. Use a small skillet and select medium-high heat to mix together the vinegar, honey, and salt. Bring to a boil. Transfer the liquid from the heat and pour it on the top of the vegetables.
3. Put the pickles aside for cooling to room temperature. Eat immediately, or refrigerate, covered, for up to 2 months.

Nutritional Value (Amount per Serving):

- Calories: 43
- Fat: 2.55g
- Carbs: 3.64g
- Protein: 1.63g

Delicious Slow Cooker Baked Potatoes

Prep Time: 5 Minutes
Cook Time: 8 Hours
Serves: 4

Ingredients:

- 4 russet potatoes, pierced all over with the tines of a fork

Directions:

1. Put the potatoes in the slow cooker. Close the lid of the appliance and set it to low heat. Cook for 8 hours.

Nutritional Value (Amount per Serving):

- Calories: 292
- Fat: 0.3g
- Carbs: 66.68g
- Protein: 7.9g

Easy Pressure Cooker Brown Rice

Prep Time: 5 Minutes
Cook Time: 15 Minutes
Serves: 6

Ingredients:

- 1 cup long-grain brown rice
- 1 cup Garden Vegetable Stock or Chicken Stock, or low-sodium store-bought vegetable or chicken stock

Directions:

1. Prepare your pressure cooker and mix together the rice and stock. Close the hood in place and set the appliance to high pressure for 15 minutes.
2. When the cook time runs out, manually release the pressure.

Nutritional Value (Amount per Serving):

- Calories: 122
- Fat: 1.04g
- Carbs: 25.44g
- Protein: 2.83g

Ratatouille As A Side Dish

Prep Time: 10 Minutes
Cook Time: 40 Minutes
Serves: 6

Ingredients:

- 1 zucchini, diced
- 1 eggplant, peeled and diced
- 1 red bell pepper, thinly sliced
- 1 fennel bulb, cored, stalks removed, bulb thinly sliced
- 1 tomato, diced
- 4 garlic cloves, minced
- 2 tablespoons extra-virgin olive oil
- ¼ teaspoon dried thyme
- ¼ teaspoon dried oregano
- ¼ cup fresh basil, chopped
- Celtic sea salt or kosher salt
- Freshly ground black pepper

Directions:

1. Preheat the oven to 350°F.
2. Use a Dutch oven to mix together the zucchini, eggplant, red bell pepper, fennel, tomato, garlic, olive oil, thyme, and oregano. Combine well for incorporated. Close the lid of the pot and bake for 40 minutes and wait the vegetables to get soft.
3. Transfer from the oven and whisk in the basil. Season to taste with salt and pepper.

Nutritional Value (Amount per Serving):

- Calories: 76
- Fat: 3.62g
- Carbs: 9.8g
- Protein: 2.62g

Crispy Roasted Brussels Sprouts With Bacon Pecans

Prep Time: 10 Minutes
Cook Time: 35 Minutes
Serves: 5

Ingredients:

- 1 pound Brussels sprouts, halved
- 4 sugar-free bacon slices, chopped
- 2 shallots, thinly sliced
- 1 teaspoon extra-virgin olive oil
- Celtic sea salt or kosher salt
- Freshly ground black pepper
- ¼ cup chopped pecans
- 1 tablespoon balsamic vinegar

Directions:

1. Preheat the oven to 400°F.
2. Put the Brussels sprouts, bacon, and shallots together on a rimmed sheet pan. Sprinkle with the olive oil and use salt and pepper for seasoning. Toss to coat.
3. Roast for around 35 minutes and wait the Brussels sprouts to get tender. Stir in the pecans and vinegar.

Nutritional Value (Amount per Serving):

- Calories: 89
- Fat: 4.28g
- Carbs: 11.35g
- Protein: 3.97g

5 Minutes Air-Fried Buffalo Cauliflower

Prep Time: 5 Minutes
Cook Time: 20 Minutes
Serves: 6

Ingredients:

- 1½ cups cauliflower florets
- ¼ cup wing sauce
- ¼ cup plain bread crumbs

Directions:

1. Prepare a large bowl to mix together the cauliflower and wing sauce. Stir to coat.
2. Spread with the bread crumbs and whisk to combine lightly. Place the cauliflower in a single layer in order within the air fryer's basket. Select fry model at 320°f for 20 minutes. Serve hot.

Nutritional Value (Amount per Serving):

- Calories: 28
- Fat: 0.58g
- Carbs: 4.68g
- Protein: 1.32g

CHAPTER 9: STAPLES & SAUCES

Super Simple Homemade Marinara

Prep Time: 5 Minutes
Cook Time: 1 Hour
Serves: 6

Ingredients:

- 2 tablespoons extra-virgin olive oil
- 1 onion, finely diced
- 8 garlic cloves, minced
- 2 (28-ounce) cans no-salt-added crushed tomatoes
- 2 tablespoons tomato paste
- 2 teaspoons dried oregano
- 2 teaspoons dried parsley

Directions:

1. Use a Dutch oven and adjust to medium heat, heat the olive oil.
2. Add the onion and garlic. Cook for 5 minutes, or until softened.
3. Add and blend together the tomatoes, tomato paste, oregano, and parsley. Stir to combine. Bring to a simmer and reduce the heat. Simmer for 1 hour to thicken. In order to achieve a smoother texture, purée the sauce with an immersion blender, or a standard blender. If not using in instance, put into refrigerator in an airtight container for at most 3 to 4 days, or freeze for less than 6 months.

Nutritional Value (Amount per Serving):

- Calories: 47
- Fat: 2.24g
- Carbs: 6.5g
- Protein: 1.25g

Yummy Chicken Stock

Prep Time: 5 Minutes
Cook Time: 25 Minutes
Serves: 1

Ingredients:

- 1 tablespoon extra-virgin olive oil
- 4 carrots, roughly chopped
- 4 celery stalks, roughly chopped
- 1 onion, roughly chopped
- 4 garlic cloves, peeled
- 2 pounds bone-in, skin-on chicken thighs or drumsticks
- 2 bay leaves
- 3 quarts water

Directions:

1. Prepare the pressure cooker and adjust to sauté. Pour in the olive oil to heat.
2. Add the carrots, celery, onion, and garlic together. Sauté for 5 minutes.
3. Add the chicken, bay leaves, and water. Close the hood in place and set the appliance to high pressure for 20 minutes.
4. When the cook time runs out, let the pressure release naturally.
5. Strain the broth and remove any solid pieces. Put them into refrigerator in an airtight container for 3 to 4 days, or freeze for no more than 6 months.

Nutritional Value (Amount per Serving):

- Calories: 3257
- Fat: 210.54g
- Carbs: 168.73g
- Protein: 174.05g

Neutral Falvored Garden Vegetable Stock

Prep Time: 10 Minutes
Cook Time: 30 Minutes
Serves: 3

Ingredients:

- 4 ounces sliced white mushrooms
- 3 carrots, roughly chopped
- 2 celery stalks, roughly chopped
- 1 onion, roughly chopped
- 1 zucchini, roughly chopped
- 4 thyme sprigs
- 2 garlic cloves, peeled
- 2 bay leaves
- 3 quarts water

Directions:

1. Prepare your pressure cooker to mix together the mushrooms, carrots, celery, onion, zucchini, thyme, garlic, bay leaves, and water. Close the hood in place and adjust the cooker to high pressure for 30 minutes.
2. When the cook time runs out, let the pressure release naturally.
3. Strain and remove any solid pieces. Put them into refrigerator in an airtight container for 3 to 4 days, or freeze for no more than 6 months.

Nutritional Value (Amount per Serving):

- Calories: 54
- Fat: 0.36g
- Carbs: 11.61g
- Protein: 2.44g

Easy Maple Barbecue Sauce

Prep Time: 5 Minutes
Cook Time: 15 Minutes
Serves: 3

Ingredients:

- 1 tablespoon extra-virgin olive oil
- 1 red onion, minced
- 4 garlic cloves, minced
- 2 cups ketchup, preferably unsweetened
- ½ cup maple syrup
- ½ cup apple cider vinegar
- 1 tablespoon Dijon mustard
- ¼ to ½ teaspoon hot sauce (optional)

Directions:

1. Use an 8-inch skillet and set at medium heat to heat the olive oil.
2. Add the red onion and garlic. Sauté for 5 minutes.
3. Whisk in the ketchup, maple syrup, vinegar, mustard, and hot sauce (if using) together. Place to a simmer and cook for 10 minutes until it gets thickened. Place them into refrigerator in an airtight container for up to 1 week.

Nutritional Value (Amount per Serving):

- Calories: 252
- Fat: 3.18g
- Carbs: 57.59g
- Protein: 1.43g

Multi-Ingredients Greek Dressing

Prep Time: 5 Minutes
Cook Time: 5 Minutes
Serves: 1

Ingredients:

- 1 cup red wine vinegar
- Juice of 2 lemons
- 8 garlic cloves, minced
- 1 tablespoon dried oregano
- ¼ cup extra-virgin olive oil
- Celtic sea salt or kosher salt
- Freshly ground black pepper

Directions:

1. Use a small bowl to stir together the vinegar, lemon juice, garlic, and oregano. Slowly and gently stir in the olive oil. Use salt and pepper for seasoning. Put them into refrigerators in an airtight container for up to 1 week.

Nutritional Value (Amount per Serving):

- Calories: 319
- Fat: 23.84g
- Carbs: 16.44g
- Protein: 2.59g

Delicious Pressure-Cooked Hard-Boiled Eggs

Prep Time: 5 Minutes
Cook Time: 5 Minutes
Serves: 6

Ingredients:

- 1 cup water
- 6 large eggs

Directions:

1. Put a wire rack as the bottom of your pressure cooker. Pour in the water. Put the eggs over the rack. Close the hood in place and adjust the appliance to High pressure for 5 minutes.
2. When the cook time runs out, make the pressure release naturally for 5 minutes before releasing any remaining pressure in a fast speed.
3. Place the eggs under cold water and wait them to get cool to the touch. Peel immediately. Wrap leftover eggs with a damp paper towel and place them into refrigerator for up to 1 week.

Nutritional Value (Amount per Serving):

- Calories: 55
- Fat: 4.51g
- Carbs: 0.61g
- Protein: 2.7g

Simple Enchilada Sauce

Prep Time: 5 Minutes
Cook Time: 5 Minutes
Serves: 2

Ingredients:

- 2 cups tomato sauce
- ½ cup Garden Vegetable Stock, or low-sodium store-bought vegetable stock
- 2 tablespoons apple cider vinegar
- 2 garlic cloves, minced
- 1 tablespoon gluten-free chili powder
- ½ teaspoon ground cumin

Directions:

1. Prepare a dutch oven and set at medium heat to stir together the tomato sauce, vegetable stock, vinegar, garlic, chili powder, and cumin. Bring to a boil. Simmer for 5 minutes until thickened slightly. Put them into refrigerators in an airtight container for around 3 to 4 days, or freeze for no more than 6 months.

Nutritional Value (Amount per Serving):

- Calories: 321
- Fat: 1.75g
- Carbs: 61.43g
- Protein: 8.25g

Bright Flavored Chimichurri Sauce

Prep Time: 10 Minutes
Cook Time: 10 Minutes
Serves: 6

Ingredients:

- 1 small shallot, minced
- 2 garlic cloves, minced
- ½ jalapeño pepper, seeded and minced
- ¼ cup finely chopped fresh cilantro
- 2 tablespoons finely chopped fresh parsley
- 1 tablespoon finely chopped fresh oregano leaves
- ¼ cup red wine vinegar
- 2 tablespoons extra-virgin olive oil
- Celtic sea salt

Directions:

1. Use a small bowl to mix together the shallot, garlic, jalapeño, cilantro, parsley, oregano, vinegar, and olive oil. Use salt as the seasoning. Stir to combine. Cover and put them into refrigerators until ready to use, or for up to 3 to 4 days.

Nutritional Value (Amount per Serving):

- Calories: 27
- Fat: 2.04g
- Carbs: 1.73g
- Protein: 0.35g

Yummy Pizza Dough

Prep Time: 10 Minutes
Cook Time: 10 Minutes
Serves: 8

Ingredients:

- 1 (¼-ounce) packet instant yeast
- 1¼ cups lukewarm water
- 1 tablespoon extra-virgin olive oil
- 2 cups all-purpose flour
- 1 cup white whole-wheat flour
- 1 teaspoon Celtic sea salt or kosher salt
- ¼ cup flaxseed meal

Directions:

1. Prepare a large bowl to mix together the yeast, water, olive oil, all-purpose and whole-wheat flours, and salt. Combine thoroughly to form a soft, sticky dough.
2. Knead in the flaxseed meal. Close the lid for the dough and let rise in a warm place for 1 around hour, or until doubled in size.
3. Separate the dough into 2 portions with plastic wrap, put them into refrigerator for up to 1 day, or freeze until ready to use. Refrigerated for less than 2 to 3 days, or frozen for no more than 6 months.

Nutritional Value (Amount per Serving):

- Calories: 207
- Fat: 3.43g
- Carbs: 37.44g
- Protein: 5.99g

Easy Pressure Cooker Beans

Prep Time: 5 Minutes
Cook Time: 25 Minutes
Serves: 6

Ingredients:

- 1 pound dried black or pinto beans
- 5 cups water, or Garden Vegetable Stock, or low-sodium store-bought vegetable stock
- 1 bay leaf
- Celtic sea salt or kosher salt

Directions:

1. Use pressure cooker to mix together the beans, water, and bay leaf. Close the hood in place and adjust the cooker to High pressure for 25 minutes. Let the pressure release naturally.
2. Transfer and eliminate the bay leaf. Season the beans with salt. Put them into refrigerator in an airtight container for around 3 to 4 days, or freeze for less than 6 months.

Nutritional Value (Amount per Serving):

- Calories: 107
- Fat: 0.81g
- Carbs: 17.85g
- Protein: 7.11g

CHAPTER 10: VEGETABLES & VEGETARIAN

Tasty Aloo GobiPotatoes and Cauliflower

Prep Time:15 Minutes
Cook Time: 40 Minutes
Serves: 4

Ingredients:

- 1 tablespoon peanut oil
- 1 teaspoon cumin seeds
- 2 cups sliced potatoes, about ¼ inch thick
- 1 teaspoon salt
- 1 teaspoon Garam Masala
- ½ teaspoon ground turmeric
- ¼ teaspoon ground cumin
- ½ teaspoon ground coriander
- ¼ teaspoon ground cayenne pepper
- ½ cup diced tomato
- ¼ cup water
- 4 cups large cauliflower florets (about 1 medium cauliflower)
- 2 teaspoons chopped fresh cilantro, for garnish (optional)

Directions:

1. Adjustto More for high heat. If the inner cooking pot is heated, pour theoil and heat until shimmering. Pour thecumin seeds and Mix. They'll sputter.
2. Pour thepotatoes and sauté, Mixring occasionally, for about 2to 3 minutes, or until they start tobrown and crisp a little.
3. Pour thesalt, garam masala, turmeric, cumin, coriander, and cayenne, and sauté for about 1 minute. Pour thetomato and water, and Mix, scraping up all the lovely fond on the bottom of the pot. Pour thecauliflower and Mixgently.
4. Lock the lid. ChooseManual and adjust the pressure to Low. Cook for about 2minutes.
5. When finished, quick-release the pressure. Open the lid.
6. Garnish with the chopped cilantro (if using).

Nutritional Value (Amount per Serving):

- Calories: 127
- Fat: 4.01g
- Carbs: 20.71g
- Protein: 4.18g

Savoury Aloo JeeraCumin-Spiced Potatoes

Prep Time:10 Minutes

Cook Time: 30 Minutes

Serves: 4

Ingredients:

- 2 cups water
- 2 cups cubed potatoes
- 1 tablespoon Ghee
- ½ serrano chile, cut into thick slices
- ½ teaspoon cumin seeds
- ¼ teaspoon ground turmeric (optional)
- 1 teaspoon salt
- ¼ cup chopped fresh cilantro, for garnish

Directions:

1. Into the inner cooking pot of the Instant Pot®, pourthe water, and place a steamer basket inside. Put the cubed potatoes in the steamer basket.
2. Lock the lid, ChooseSteam, and high pressure. Cook for around 6minutes. When finished, quick-release the pressure.
3. Unlock and Remove thelid. Remove thesteamer basket and set the potatoes aside. Rinse and dry the inner liner. Place it back into the Instant Pot®.
4. Adjusting to More for high heat. After the pot is hot, pour theghee and heat . Pour theserrano pepper and cumin seeds, and let the seeds sputter and cook .
5. Pour theturmeric (if using) and Mixto mix. Pour thepotatoes and salt, and mix gently to coat the potatoes with the flavored ghee, being carefulto not break them.
6. Garnish with the cilantro and serve.

Nutritional Value (Amount per Serving):

- Calories: 167
- Fat: 6.76g
- Carbs: 13.8g
- Protein: 13.21g

Home-Made Bundh Gobi MutterCabbage and Peas

Prep Time:15 Minutes
Cook Time: 35 Minutes
Serves: 4

Ingredients:

- 1 tablespoon peanut oil
- ¼ teaspoon cumin seeds
- 2 teaspoons minced garlic
- 1 teaspoon minced ginger
- ½ cup thinly sliced red onion
- ¼ teaspoon ground turmeric
- 3 cups chopped cabbage
- ¼ cup water
- Salt
- ½ cup fresh or frozen green peas
- Chopped fresh cilantro, for garnish

Directions:

1. Adjusting to More for high heat. If the inner cooking pot is heated, pour theoil and heat . Pour thecumin seeds and cook for about 1 minute, or until they start sputtering.
2. Pour thegarlic and ginger. Let it all cook together for about half a minute. Pour theonion and sauté until brown and crisp at the edges, about 5 minutes. Pour theturmeric and let it mix into the oil.
3. Pour thecabbage, water, and salt. Mixto combine.
4. Lock the lid. ChooseManual and high pressure. Cook for about 1 minute.
5. When finished, quick-release the pressure.
6. Pour thepeas and mix fullyto heat them through.
7. Garnish with the cilantro.

Nutritional Value (Amount per Serving):

- Calories: 242
- Fat: 18.9g
- Carbs: 7.94g
- Protein: 11.32g

Savoury Baingan BhartaSmoky Mashed Eggplant

Prep Time:15 Minutes
Cook Time: 50 Minutes
Serves: 4

Ingredients:

- 1 medium eggplant, peeled, cut in half, and then sliced lengthwise
- ⅓cup vegetable oil
- 3 cloves garlic, minced
- ½ onion, diced
- ¼ teaspoon ground turmeric
- ⅛ teaspoon ground cayenne pepper
- ½ teaspoon salt, plus more to taste
- ⅓cup diced tomatoes
- ½ cup water
- ¼ teaspoon liquid smoke
- 2 tablespoons chopped cilantro

Directions:

1. Preheat the Instant Pot by choosing Sauté and adjust to More for high heat. Pourin a few tablespoons of oil and heat until shimmering. Add one layer of eggplant slices. Let them cook until charred on the bottom. If you move them before they arecharred, you won't get the smoky taste you need.
2. Once these slices char, scrape up the char from the bottom. Then Pour thenext batch of eggplant slices, and more oil, as necessary. Scrape the char between batches. It should take about 15 minutes to get all of the eggplant slices charred.
3. Once the eggplant is charred, add in the garlic, onion, turmeric, cayenne, and salt. Let the spices roast in the oil for about 1 minute.
4. Pour thetomatoes and scrape up all the brown bits from the bottom of the pot. Pour thewater.
5. Lock the lid. ChooseManual and high pressure. Cook for about 3minutes.

6. When finished, use the quick method to release the pressure.

7. Open the lidand carefully open the pot. If there is too much liquid in the pot, shooseSauté and simmer until the liquid evaporates. (It will thicken as it cools.)

8. Pour theliquid smoke and Mixwell. Garnish with the cilantro and enjoy withnaan.

Nutritional Value (Amount per Serving):

- Calories: 202
- Fat: 18.28g
- Carbs: 10.85g
- Protein: 1.8g

Quick Coconut-Tomato Soup

Prep Time:10 Minutes
Cook Time: 40 Minutes
Serves: 4

Ingredients:

- 1 can coconut milk
- 1 red onion, diced
- 6 large tomatoes, cut into quarters
- ¼ cup chopped fresh cilantro
- 1 teaspoon minced garlic
- 1 teaspoon minced ginger
- 1 teaspoon salt
- ½ teaspoon ground cayenne pepper
- 1 teaspoon ground turmeric
- 1 tablespoon agave nectar or honey

Directions:

1.Combineall of the ingredients.
2.Lock the lid. ChooseManual and high pressure. Cook for about 5minutes.
3.When finished, let the pressure release. Open the lid.
4.Using an immersion blender, blend thesoup until smooth, and enjoy.

Nutritional Value (Amount per Serving):

- Calories: 343
- Fat: 27.66g
- Carbs: 25.19g
- Protein: 5.58g

Tasty Marathi KadhiTangy Yogurt Soup

Prep Time:10 Minutes
Cook Time: 40 Minutes
Serves: 4

Ingredients:

- 1 cup full-fat yogurt (you can substitute soy yogurt)
- 2 cups water
- 1 teaspoon salt
- 1 teaspoon sugar
- ¼ teaspoon ground cayenne pepper
- 4 tablespoons chickpea flour
- 1 tablespoon Ghee or coconut oil
- 1 teaspoon black mustard seeds
- 1 teaspoon cumin seeds
- 1 serrano chile, thinly sliced
- 1 tablespoon minced ginger
- 1 teaspoon ground turmeric

Directions:

1. In a medium bowl, whisk together the yogurt, water, salt, sugar, cayenne, and chickpea flour untilcompletely mixed. (Don't let it get too frothy.) Put aside.
2. Adjusting to More for high heat. If the inner cooking pot is heated, pour theghee and heat . Pour themustard seeds and cumin seeds and let them sputter for about 10to 20 seconds.
3. Pour theserrano chile, ginger, and turmeric. Addin the yogurt mixture and mixto combine.
4. Lock the lid. Choosethe Soup setting and high pressure. Cook for around 6minutes.
5. When finished, let the pressure releasefor about 10minutes, then quick-release any remaining pressure. Open the lid, Mixwell, and enjoy withrice

or a side of your choice.

Nutritional Value (Amount per Serving):

- Calories: 199
- Fat: 12.24g
- Carbs: 12.75g
- Protein: 11.23g

Quick Marathi RassaMixed Vegetables with Coconut

Prep Time:15 Minutes
Cook Time: 35 Minutes
Serves: 6

Ingredients:

- ¼ cup unsweetened shredded coconut
- ½ cup hot water, divided, plus additional as needed
- 1 onion, chopped
- 2 tomatoes, chopped
- 4 garlic cloves, minced
- 1 tablespoon minced ginger
- ¼ cup chopped fresh cilantro
- ½ teaspoon ground cumin
- ½ teaspoon ground turmeric
- ¼ teaspoon ground cayenne pepper
- 1 teaspoon salt
- 1 tablespoon peanut oil
- 5 to 6 cups mixed vegetables, chopped into large pieces

Directions:

1. In a blender jar or a food-processor bowl, pour thecoconut and cover it with ¼ cup of hot water. Let the coconut hydrate for about 10 minutes. (While it hydrates, you can prep the other things.)
2. To the coconut, pour theonion, tomatoes, garlic, ginger, cilantro,turmeric, cayenne, and salt. Process to a smooth purée. Add more water as necessary, but use as little as possible.
3. Adjusting to More for high heat. If the inner cooking pot is heated, pour theoil and heat until it smokes slightly, then Pour thecoconut-onion-tomato mixture.
4. Let the mixture cook, without Mixring, until most of the water has evaporated, 3 to 5 minutes. Mixfullyso that it cooks equallyand begins

tolose its fresh green color, about another 2 minutes.

5.Pour thechopped vegetables and the remaining ¼ cup of water and Mixto combine.

6.Lock the lid. ChooseManual and adjust the pressure to Low. Cook for about 3minutes.

7.When finished, quick-release the pressure.

8.Unlock and Remove thelid. Addmore salt as necessary. enjoy withnaan, chapatis, or over rice.

Nutritional Value (Amount per Serving):

- Calories: 103
- Fat: 4.03g
- Carbs: 14.81g
- Protein: 2.62g

APPENDIX RECIPE INDEX